Sacred Stories

Sacred Dreams:

Bible Myth and Metaphor

Sacred Stories

Sacred Dreams:

Bible Myth and Metaphor

Edward V. Tuttle

Pathways of Light
Santa Maria, California

Publisher's Cataloging-in-Publication
(Provided by Quality Books, Inc.)

Tuttle, Edward V.
    Sacred stories, sacred dreams : Bible myth and
metaphor. Volume I / by Edward V. Tuttle. -- 1st ed.
    p. cm.
    Includes bibliographical references.
    ISBN 0-9716484-3-3

    1. Metaphor in the Bible. 2. Bible--Criticism,
interpretation, etc. 3. Jesus Christ--Biography.
I. Title.

BS511.3.T88 2002   220.6
                       QBI33-269

ACKNOWLEDGMENTS

That we stand on the shoulders of all those who have gone before is an acknowledgment of the first order. The Metaphysical Bible Dictionary, the patient and illumined work of Charles Fillmore, was an invaluable source of Biblical name origin and definitions. The works of authors Ervin Seale, Robert A. Johnson, and John A. Sanford, inspired the approach. I am grateful to the people of Pathways Community Church, in Santa Maria, who first heard the stories from the pulpit and encouraged me to write a book. And yet it might never have been written had not my friend, and coach, Anna Dargitz, challenged me to set aside time each day to write. I thank Joanne Blum, James Gunn, Anne Kollath, and William Alarid, who read early drafts and spurred me on. And finally, as predictable and welcome as each day's sunrise, there was the steadfast love and encouragement of my soul mate, my wife, Linda.

A Note to the Reader

The narrative throughout is broken into chapters and appears in this typeface. Those portions of the work that contain contemplative and interpretative comments appear in a distinctly different typeface. For those who wish, this allows for the narrative portions to be read from beginning to end without pausing to consider the interpretive comments offered by the author. The objective throughout is to stimulate the reader's imagination and intuition for determining how the story, viewed as metaphor, relates to their own life and experience.

Let the words of my mouth
and the meditation of my heart
be acceptable in thy sight, O God.
(Psalm 19:14)

Thou dost show me the path of life;
in thy presence there is fullness of joy,
in thy right hand are pleasures forever more.
(Psalm 16:11)

Contents

INTRODUCTION

"No one's story exists alone," writes Daniel Taylor in *The Healing Power of Stories,* *"each is tangled up in countless others. Pull a thread in your story and feel the tremor half a world and two millennia away. Without you and your story I cannot know my story and myself."*

Whenever a story comes alive in the mind and heart of the reader, or listener, a personal connection takes place, and for a time they *become* the hero or heroine. They feel and move with them through the story to its final resolution, and in the process they often find that they have learned something about life, and how it may be lived. Unless a story captures the reader or listener in this way it remains a pale bloodless tale of little importance, quickly forgotten. It is the aim of this book, the first in a projected series, to awaken in the reader a similar connection with selected stories from the Bible.

The Bible may well be the least read, and even less understood, *best seller* in the entire world of books. Common reactions to it range from a blind acceptance of it as the unchangeable and irrefutable word of God, to those who find it too hard to read, unbelievable, and essentially irrelevant. The former cannot, or will not, question it, while the latter are likely to dismiss it out of hand. They each miss the power of it to kindle the imagination and to nourish the soul, for they each fail to see it as *their* story.

Modern translations have done little to address the needs of either group, and in the process of making the Bible more readable they have stripped it of much of its poetic power and beauty. *Sacred Stories, Sacred Dreams: Bible Myth and Metaphor* presents scriptural stories and events in a way that makes the Bible more user-friendly, more personal to the reader, and as relevant as today's headlines.

THE SUNDAY CHALLENGE

For more than two decades, with very few exceptions, every Sunday has found me in the pulpit of a church sharing familiar stories and events from the Bible. The ever-present challenge was to tell the old familiar stories in a way that would bring a new light of understanding, even excitement, to the mind and life of those gathered before me. To achieve this result the story had to be told in a way that would allow the listener to connect with it, to hear and see the story as being relevant to their life -- to recognize it as their story. It was this challenge that brought me back Sunday after Sunday, and gave birth to this book.

Jesus encountered the same problem, even when teaching his disciples. *"Do you have eyes, and fail to see? Do you have ears, and fail to hear?"* He asked them. (Mark 8:18) His cry of frustration at their lack of understanding, of insight, concerning the principles he taught, he might well cry out today. His solution was to wrap the truth in story, for he knew the special power of story to reach past the intellectual, the conceptual, to that deeper level of mind where image and symbol is the universal language spoken.

His favorite story form was the parable; two stories placed side by side. The first was always about the activities and objects of daily life, things with which his listeners were familiar, like fishing, or planting a crop, or building a house. It was about real people engaged in the affairs that filled their days, but his intent was that they see beyond the literal story to the broader truth hidden within. The parable was to serve as a metaphor that pointed to a deeper truth, a principle by which one might *"have life and have it more abundantly."* Its purpose was to evoke a connection with their life experience, to open their eyes to new ways of being and acting in their world. In this way it would become their story.

But fortunately, the parable is not the only form of story to have this illuminating effect. Mythology, folk tales, Aesops fables, even our nightly dreams, all contain archetypal themes and images common to man throughout time.

13

All have the power to reach past the surface intellect to deeper layers of mind and understanding in the individual, where they find resonance and life.

THE SOLUTION

It was an appreciation of this fact that provided the element to solve my Sunday challenge, for much of the Bible is not about ordinary things happening to ordinary people. It is about angelic visits, virgin births, miraculous healing, walking on water, the parting of a sea, a whale that regurgitates a live man after three days, and more. This is the stuff of myths and dreams where image is paramount, and the language spoken is that of symbol and metaphor. Here was the answer to my Sunday challenge. I would suggest that my listeners hear the story as if it were a dream they had, in which all the characters, places and objects, were some part of their consciousness, their psyche. What could be more personal?

WHY DREAMS?

There is elegance to the manner in which our unconscious dream-producing mind communicates with our conscious waking mind by presenting the drama in the language of symbol and metaphor. Some dream episodes present the intended message for the dreamer with great clarity. For example, I remember a dream I had in which I was shot in the back of the head. I remember feeling the muzzle of the gun against the base of my skull, when the shot was fired. The dream began and ended with that image. I was instantly awake, and relieved that it was just a dream. Aware that everything in the dream serves as a metaphor, including the overall drama itself, I lay awake letting the dream images sharpen in my mind and wondered what message it had for me. The answer came with blinding clarity.

The previous evening I had begun to listen to a tape that was laden with subliminal messages that would allegedly improve my life in some important way, which now escapes me. I had felt a sense of unease about the program, but had listened to a portion of the first tape. The dream message was clear and relevant. Someone I could not see, and could not identify, had shot me in the back of my head. The bullet entered my brain, but I was not killed. It was a perfect metaphor for my listening to a tape laced with subliminal suggestions while ignorant of the source, or the content. Not a wise thing to do. The elegant economy of image in the dream made it all the more powerful. The message was heard, the decision easy. It would be best to not welcome either experience.

INTRODUCTION

Bible stories and events are filled with a similar elegance and economy of image, symbol and metaphor, and like our personal dreams will reveal the messages that they hold for our life when we open to it.

The Talmud suggests that an unexamined dream is like an unopened letter. The Bible for many, and for too long, has remained an "unopened letter." In *Sacred Stories, Sacred Dreams: Bible Myth and Metaphor*, we invite the reader to take a fresh look at biblical stories and events with the same curiosity they would apply to a dream they had. What awaits the reader is the joy and wonder of discovering their own truth reflected in the drama.

THE METHOD

We found that when we viewed biblical stories and events through the lens of metaphor and symbol, exploring their mythic dimensions as we would the drama and content of our nocturnal dreams, they spoke to us in new and exciting ways. This provided the desired connection, for our dreams are written and produced in the same symbolic language that we find in the Bible. It would be as though the story began with the words, "I had a dream." It changed the context from something "out there" into an inner experience where the drama and characters became personal and alive within us. When we recognized that everything and everyone in the dream-story was some part of our own psyche, or state of mind, then we could begin to see its relevance in our life. The dream-story was no longer an unopened letter, we could see it for what it was -- *our* story.

And a deeper connection is revealed, for our psyche is not an isolated bit of mental/emotional flotsam floating aimlessly and unconnected in the Great Ocean of Consciousness. Our psyche is some part of the Wholeness of whatever It (God) is, and is inhabited by archetypal energy patterns that are universal in all people, and all cultures, throughout time. We are, like it or not, more alike in our essential nature than we might realize. This journey into the mythic dimensions of the Bible, this search for our story, can be as intriguing and challenging as a fine mystery tale. After all, it deals with the mystery of mysteries -- God, and God's relationship with man.

THE PROCESS

The process begins with determining the meaning of the name of the character, or place. This provides us with an important clue to their basic nature and how that plays into the drama. Jerusalem, for example, means *place of peace,* and Judah means *place of praise and prayer.* These are actual destinations for characters in the story, but they also are effective as metaphors for identifiable places in consciousness, in the inner life of the individual, and also work as such in the story. The Unity Metaphysical Dictionary, published by Unity School of Ministry, Lee's Summit, Missouri, is an excellent source for this information. This work of Charles Fillmore, founder of Unity, is an invaluable source for any study of this kind.

The process invites the maximum play of our intuitive nature as we appreciate that each image, each symbol, as well as the overall drama, offers a view of our inner world and its relation to that which is at work in the outer. Except that here, as we examine biblical stories in their mythical dimensions, we reverse the method and look at the outer as a parable, or metaphor, to the inner state of consciousness at play in the drama.

THIS VOLUME

Sacred Stories, Sacred Dreams: Bible Myth and Metaphor, is based on the story of Jesus the Christ, from his birth to his death and resurrection, and presents him as the Great Example rather than the Great Exception. As the Great Example he becomes a Teacher and Guide, who says, *"Take my yoke (yoga) upon you, and learn from me."* (Matt. 11.29) His life and teaching are an example of the living truth of the dual nature of man, *"made in the image and likeness of God"* and yet created out of the dust of the earth. For we are both human and divine, but in the experiencing our humanity we tend to forget our divinity, our essential spiritual nature. This story has the power to remind us. And in our remembering we may come to realize that it is not simply a story about a most remarkable man, but one that tells of a dimension of spiritual awareness that lies like a seed in the heart of every living soul. It is a story about the birth, the growth, and the full flowering of that seed in *you*. It is -- *your* story.

In crafting the story, I have taken the liberty of putting a bit of flesh on the bare bones of scripture in order to bring the characters to life, to make them easier to identify with, and to make the tale more readable. Also each section of the story is followed with some thoughts as to the lessons to be drawn from symbolic language used in the story. What lesson or principle is revealed? What light does it shed on our lives? And though examples are offered, they are not intended to be exhaustive. It is to arouse in the reader a playful curiosity of mind as to how the story or event may relate metaphorically to her life. Our intent is to take the Bible seriously but not literally, and in doing so to reveal the story within the story. This is the realm in which we play throughout our journey together

CONCERNING MYTHS

Concerning myths and their value in our lives, Robert A. Johnson, in his books *He,* and *She,* writes.

"Myths are a rich source of psychological insight. They are a special kind of literature not written or created by a single individual, but produced by the imagination and experience of an entire age and culture and can be seen as the distillation of the dreams and experiences of a whole culture.

"Myths portray a collective image, they tell us about things that are true for all people. The details of the story may be unverifiable or even fantastic, but actually a myth is profoundly and universally true. Myths depict levels of reality that include the outer rational world as well as the less understood inner world." (*She*, p x – xi) (7)

"We must remember that a myth is a living entity, and exists within every person. You will get the true living form of the myth if you can see it as it spins away inside yourself. The most rewarding mythological experience you can have is to see how it lives in your own psychological structure" (*He*, p. x). (6)

A myth is indeed a living entity, and there is a mythological dimension to every life, as there is to every culture and every age. To view the stories of the Bible in their mythological dimensions does not lessen the beauty or sacredness of the text, but opens a window that offers a different view of the landscape, a landscape we may ultimately recognize as our own -- sacred story, sacred dream.

AN INVITATION

Now let us together stroll leisurely through the story, tasting the words and welcoming the images they evoke, as though for the first time. Then, with the innocence and openhearted curiosity of a child, let us hold the drama and its symbolic language, up to the light of our intuition. Echoing the opening words of Proverbs, let us seek to "know wisdom, understand words of insight, and receive instruction in wise dealing, righteousness, justice, and equity." (Proverbs 1.2)

While we remember that all the characters and places live within us, let us humbly ask the story to reveal its timeless wisdom, its truth and guidance, and to do it in a way that is relevant to life, and to the purposeful, powerful, living of it. On the surface it is the story of the people, places, and events in the life of Jesus from his conception to his death and resurrection. It is also the story of the conception of the Christ in you, and in every living soul.

"The kingdom of God is spread upon the earth and men do not see it."
                                        Joseph Campbell

PART I

HEAVEN-SENT

This is the story of conception and birth of a man-child, but more than that it is about the birth of a new concept, a new dimension of awareness in man/woman – the Christ. And it is your story.

" ... and his name shall be called Immanuel – God with us." (Matt. 1.23)

HEAVEN SENT

Long ago and far away,
There was a wondrous event.
A child was born to common folk,
Some said was Heaven-sent.

Angels sang, shepherds watched,
Gifts the Wise Men brought.
They saw a star in the eastern skies
And seeing it, they thought -

We'll go and see what this portends,
This star—so still and bright.
And traveling down to Bethlehem town,
They came on the strangest sight.

In a place where cattle were kept
they found, a new born babe, a boy.
Seeing the child, and the light round about
Their hearts were filled with great joy.

For there in a manger lay the Son of Man,
Reflecting God's infinite love,
The eternal promise of peace on earth
They'd looked for, from heaven above.

But, it's in the heart of man to be found.
This peace—this blessed event.
And it's born anew with the birth of each child,
For each is heaven-sent.

E. V. Tuttle

CHAPTER 1

The Conception

She was young, not yet sixteen, when it happened — an event destined to change the course of mankind forever. It happened at night, in the wee small hours of the morning, a time when we are most open and vulnerable. She heard voice, *"Greetings favored one! The Lord is with you."* (Luke 1:28) The words entered her mind like the low rumble of distant thunder, and she was instantly awake. At the foot of her bed stood a towering presence, a figure that seemed to radiate a light from within. Startled, she clutched the bed clothes close around her. It was the angel Gabriel who stood before her. He spoke softly, his voice deep, calming. She was troubled and confused by the greeting, but somehow reassured by the voice.

Gabriel said, *"Do not be afraid, Mary, for you have found favor with God, and now, you*

25

will conceive in your womb and bear a son, and you will name him Jesus." Mary, convinced that she was dreaming, shook her head in an effort to awaken. Gabriel continued, *"He will be great, and will be called the Son of the Most High, and the Lord God will give to him the throne of his ancestor David. He will reign over the house of Jacob forever, and of his kingdom there will be no end."* (Luke 1.33)

Mary, satisfied now that she was awake, was astonished at this unbelievable declaration. Considering it highly unlikely she asked, "How shall this be, since I have no husband?" For though she was promised in marriage to a local carpenter named Joseph, she had not been with him, or any man. She was a virgin.

Gabriel, who had even more astonishing news replied, *"The Holy Spirit will come upon you, and the power of the Most High will over-shadow you; therefore the child to be born will be holy; he will be called Son of God."* (Luke 1.35) And by way of proof he added, *"And now, your kinswoman Elizabeth in her old age has also conceived a son; and this is the sixth month for her who was said to be barren. For nothing will be impossible with God."* (Luke 1.37) Filled with awe and wonder, Mary accepted the word of Gabriel, and said, *"Behold, I am the handmaid of the Lord; let it be to me according to your word."*

(Luke 1.38) His mission complete, the angel Gabriel vanished into the darkness.

Sleep was out of the question. Mary stared into the darkness, darker still in the absence of the radiance of her visitor. His words echoed in her mind, resonated with something deep within her soul. She felt so incredibly alive! What had just happened? Was it just a dream, or could it be -- a miracle? Since earliest childhood she had heard tales of the prophecy that foretold of the birth of a Messiah, who would one day rise up and lead her people to freedom and greatness. Could it possibly be? And was it true that Elizabeth was with child at her age? Unbelievable!

At first light she arose from her bed and quickly dressed. She wrapped her cloak close about her against the morning chill, and hurried into the hill country, to the city of Judah, *place of prayer and praise*. There she entered the house of Zachariah and Elizabeth who, according to the angel Gabriel, had experienced their own miracle, and to her amazement found it to be true. For it was obvious that Elizabeth had indeed miraculously conceived.

Now Zachariah, which means *praise the Lord*, was a priest, as had been his father, and his grandfather, and his male ancestors reaching back to the time of Moses, and the beginning of Judaism's formal priesthood. He was happy being a priest, had been born to it, and for the past three decades he had served God in His temple. The only sadness that he felt, that lay like stone upon his heart, was the fact that his beloved Elizabeth had failed to give him a son to follow in his footsteps. With Elizabeth now well past her fortieth year, he had finally given up hope, and was resigned to what he felt must be the will of God. But then suddenly, miraculously, that had all changed one night when he was on duty in the temple.

It was six months prior to Gabriel's nocturnal encounter with Mary, when he visited Zachariah with a message from God that was just as startling, and as unbelievable, as that which he later delivered to Mary. It happened while the priest was on duty in the temple. According to the custom it fell to Zachariah by lot to enter the temple of the Lord to light the incense. There was a large crowd outside, praying at the same hour. Zachariah was completely absorbed in the routine of a ritual he had performed thousands of times, when suddenly he became aware of an angel of the Lord standing on the right side of the altar. He was startled, and a wave of fear swept over him.

The angel said to him, *"Do not be afraid Zachariah for your prayer is heard and your wife Elizabeth will bear you a son, and you shall call his name John.* (Luke 1.13)   Gabriel, who saw that Zachariah was numb with shock, spoke of the joy that the birth of John would bring to him and Elizabeth, and to many. He spoke of John's nature and future, saying, *"He will be great before the Lord, and filled with the Holy Spirit, even from his mother's womb."* And of John's mission, saying, *"He will turn many of the sons of Israel to the Lord their God, and he will go before him in the spirit and power of Elijáh, to make ready for the Lord a people prepared."*(Luke 1.17)

Zachariah could not believe what he was seeing and hearing. He asked, *"How shall I know this? For I am an old man, and my wife is advanced in years."* Only now does the angel identify himself, saying, I am Gabriel, *"who stands in the presence of God, who brings you the good news."* (Luke 1.19) But because of Zachariah's disbelief, Gabriel told him that he would be *"silent and unable to speak until the day these things come to pass."* (Luke 1:20) His message delivered, Gabriel departed.

Visibly shaken by the experience, Zachariah could hardly stand. He was stunned. Hope and doubt struggled within him. Was it real, what he had just experienced? Could it be that his Elizabeth was actually going to be with child? Hope, coupled with a long-held desire, gained the ascendancy within his breast as the promise of the angel Gabriel echoed in his heart. He would at last have a son, and not just any child, but one destined to be a spiritual leader like Elijah. One with the awesome mission of calling many of the sons of Israel to the Lord their God, to make ready for the Lord a people prepared. Pray God that it is true, he thought. If there was ever a time to praise God, with whom all things are possible, now was such a time. But when he opened his mouth, no sound came forth. He was unable to utter a single word. When he came out of the temple he could not speak to those who were still there. He was only able to make signs to them, but they saw that something unusual had happened to him in the temple.

As he walked homeward thoughts of Elizabeth filled his mind, and mixed with the glow of what had just happened to him. When he thought of his wife, Elizabeth, words from Proverbs came to mind, *"a good wife who can find? She is far more precious than jewels."* (Proverbs 31.10)

Descended from Aaron, Moses' brother and Israel's first high priest, her devotion to God was deep and abiding. They had both consecrated their lives to God, a fact that only increased the sadness they felt at being childless. But who could know the mind of God, that infinite and unknowable Presence? And what could he tell her of what had just happened in the temple?

When he arrived home, and could not speak a word, Elizabeth was s frightened and asked what was wrong. By signs, he was able to assure her that he was not ill but did not share anything about his experience in the temple. If the angel had spoken true, it would all be revealed in time. If not, he did not want Elizabeth to suffer yet one more crushing disappointment. And praise God, his Elizabeth did conceive.

He would never forget that moment, when Elizabeth, breathless with joy and wonder, tears streaming down her radiant face, had cried, "Praise God, our prayers are answered. I am with child." He could not speak, but he had tears to match her own as he took her into his arms and held her close. His heart was filled with love, and from his soul there arose a silent prayer of joy and thanksgiving.

Her joy was magnified when Zachariah revealed what had taken place in the temple. While the new life quickened in her, Elizabeth remained silent to the world, and hid the fact of her pregnancy from everyone at large for five months. Her failure through the years to have a child, a failure that she suffered in silence, had made her an object of unspoken pity and reproach among many in the community. She would not, could not, reveal the miracle that had taken place until the pregnancy was well developed. Such a revelation would only have been met with disbelief. She had just begun her third trimester when Mary arrived with her own startling news.

Elizabeth had seen her approach and stood at the open doorway, her arms extended in greeting. With a happy cry, Mary rushed into the embrace. Elizabeth, her face radiant with joy, said, *"When I heard your greeting, the babe in my womb leaped for joy."* (Luke 1.41) A sense of relief flooded over Mary, as she nestled in those strong and comforting arms. And she now had proof that the angel Gabriel had spoken the truth concerning Elizabeth. She was most assuredly with child.

Elizabeth gently placed her fingers under Mary's chin and lifted her face so that she might look into her eyes, and asked, "What has brought you here child?" Mary's eyes filled with tears, and with a mixture of wonder and fear, the story of her own encounter with the angel Gabriel poured from her lips.

Exhausted at last, and clinging fiercely to Elizabeth's comforting arms, she whispered, I don't know what to do? Elizabeth held her at arm length. "Do?" She said. "You're going to have something to eat, and then you're going to rest. I want you to stay with us for a time. We have plenty of room. You can stay here as long as you want." And then she added, almost as though she was speaking to herself, *"And blessed is she who believed that there would be a fulfillment of what was spoken to her from the Lord."* (Luke 1.45)

Mary had found the comfort and confirmation that she was seeking, and the spiritual support that she so desperately needed. She stayed with Elizabeth for three months before returning home, long enough to be present at the birth of John, he who was to become John the Baptist. But we get ahead of our story. What of Joseph, the potential bridegroom, how did he react to the news about Mary?

His reaction was not surprising. He was stunned, speechless. He could not believe it. How could this possibly happen? How could she do this to him, his sweet Mary? They had such dreams of their future together. Anger and hurt surged through him in tormenting, overwhelming waves. Devastated, he felt ill. He must think! Think! What was he to do now?

He had loved Mary from the moment he first saw her, walking in the marketplace. When had she become a young woman? He knew the family, and had been vaguely aware of her as a gangling child on the verge of adolescence. But the vision of grace and beauty that he saw that day in the marketplace so completely captured him that he spoke to her father that very evening. And it was arranged that she would become his wife.

But what was he to do now? He would not be made a fool of, nor would he do anything to shame Mary. Painful as it might be, for he still loved her, a *"quiet divorce"* appeared to be the only solution. (Matt. 1:19) Even this had its pitfalls. Joseph was well known in the region, and held in high regard. He was a fine craftsman, carpenter and builder, and he was also of the house and lineage of King David. It was no secret that Mary was his betrothed. How would he ever explain a quiet divorce? Under the circumstances, was there any possibility of such? While he was considering all of this, an angel of the Lord appeared to him in a dream and said, *"Joseph, son of David, do not be afraid to take Mary as your wife for that which is conceived in her is of the Holy Spirit. She will bear a son, and you shall name him Jesus."* (Matt. 1:20)

Here was a perfect solution, for the situation would fulfill a prophecy spoken by Isaiah. *"Behold, a young woman shall conceive and bear a son, and shall call his name Immanuel, which means, God is with us."* (Isaiah 7.14) (Note: Matthew, referring to this prophecy changed "young woman" to "virgin." Matt. 1:23)

When Joseph awoke, he did as the angel of the Lord commanded him. He went searching for Mary, and found her in seclusion at the home of Zachariah and Elizabeth. Mary, uncertain at first, found in Joseph's eyes what she had hoped to see and rushed into his arms.

As he held her he told her of his dream, of his love for her, and of the decision he had reached. He felt that they should be married at once. Mary told him that she felt that she should remain with Elizabeth for a time, and Joseph agreed. Three months had passed when word reached Joseph that Elizabeth had given birth to a son, who Zachariah had named John. It was then that Joseph took Mary as his wife, but *"knew her not until she had borne a son; and he called his name Jesus."* (Matt. 1.25)

THE CONCEPTION PRINCIPLE

The story is about the birth of a man-child, but it is also about the birth of a new dimension of consciousness, a new concept of man, and of his relationship to God and to his fellow man. It is about the Christ, or Christ consciousness, a dimension of spiritual awareness that realizes and declares a personal relationship with God, like that of a son to a father, *"The Father and I are one."* (John 1.30)

It is a dimension of spiritual awareness that is not confined only to those who identify themselves as Christians. The Christ, from the Greek Christos, means the anointed one, and points to something universal. It is a way of being in the world that lies as a seed in the heart of every living soul, an inherent potential that is universal in

35

all of mankind. This is the Conception, and it is everyone's story.

MARY

The birth of anything always begins with a conception, a movement in consciousness, a thought or idea. A concept, an idea, is an invisible miraculous thing in itself, and like a single sperm searching for an egg; it seeks a nurturing lodging place. In the story it finds what it seeks in Mary, but even here the welcome, the connection, is tenuous. "How shall this be, since I have no husband?" she asked, expressing her doubts and fears. Gabriel's reply that the Holy Spirit would come upon her, and the power of God overshadows her, seemed beyond her comprehension. It was not until he offered as proof word of the miraculous pregnancy of her elderly relative Elizabeth that she accepted the possibility of the promise he brought. We do not find it easy to accept the possibility of miracles in our life.

Though Mary found it hard to believe Gabriel's message, she was young and innocent, a time of life when nothing seems to be impossible. Her faith and openness win out, and her response to Gabriel's incredible message is one of acceptance; "let it be with me according to your word." (Luke 1.38)

Gabriel's word that the Holy Spirit, (the Wholeness of Spirit), would come upon her, and the Most High overshadow her, held a power and promise that could not be denied. Within the spiritual depths of Mary a new concept of man was awakened, one who *"will be great, and will be called the Son of the Most High."* (Luke 1.32) A new dimension of consciousness was conceived, a new concept of man was to be brought forth.

Within us there lives a Mary, a part of our consciousness that remains virginal, chaste and innocent, untouched by the world and its affairs. She is the essence of the feminine, the soul in our consciousness, open and receptive, vulnerable and willing. Only this sacred space within our being can supply the womb for carrying the conception of the Christ within.

The point of conception is decision time, and the powers in play can go either way. At times fear, one is likely to call it being reasonable, wins out and the question "How can this be?" is answered with "It can't!" The risk and uncertainty is more than one is ready to accept and the possibility withers and dies. But sometimes our Mary, the innocent trusting visionary who is alive and well within us carries the day, and the concept, like the fertilized egg, takes root. But the struggle, internal or external, has just begun.

ELIZABETH

The story suggests that the conception of the Christ requires a young, innocent, trusting soul to accept and carry the seed. What then is the nature of the consciousness that is to conceive and give birth to John, who is destined to become John, the Baptist? John was to fulfill the prophetic role of one who is to "prepare the way of the Lord," to make ready a people for the coming of the Christ.

Elizabeth was past the usual childbearing age and was barren. To be barren is to appear to be incapable of producing or sustaining life, much like a desert in winter. But anyone who has seen a desert burst forth with teeming life at the touch of rain realizes that the appearance is misleading.

Elizabeth, which means *consecrated to GoJ*, had for years suffered silently a feeling of emptiness at her failure to produce a child, but she remained strong in her faith. And though, like the desert, she appeared barren her soul was rich with the unborn potential of a life consecrated to God. Here was a strong and mature soul, a descendant of Aaron the brother of Moses, who was the first in the line of formal priests of Israel. Had she been a man she would have been a priest. She had not given up hope; she remained ready, consecrated. It was Zachariah who required the visit by the angel Gabriel, for it was he who had resigned himself to things as they appeared.

ZACHARIAH

Zachariah is old, and his innocence is long gone, when he is visited by the angel Gabriel and told that Elizabeth will conceive and bear a son, who Zachariah will name John. He finds this hard to believe. *"For I am an old man, and my wife is getting on in years."* (Luke 1.18) It flies in the face of reason, and we all know that, like oil and water, reason and miracles do not mix.

But Gabriel has a reply that we each might consider carefully if we are at all interested in entertaining miracles in our lives. It has to do with the way in which Gabriel identifies himself as one who *"stands in the presence of God."* We become Gabriel-like when we choose to stand in the presence of God, to place our faith and trust utterly and completely in God. This is an identity that is open to miracles; "For with God nothing will be impossible." (Luke 1.37) Gabriel resolves the problem of Zachariah's disbelief by striking him dumb.

Zachariah wants to believe the message that Gabriel has brought, even though it flies in face of reason. Though the heart wants it to be true, the intellect shouts it is impossible, unreasonable, and in the absence of faith the intellect wins and another dream dies. But Zachariah is a man of faith, perhaps he has seen the desert bloom, and his faith is reinforced when Gabriel takes away his ability to give voice to his doubts by striking him dumb.

His being struck dumb is a necessary element in the tale, and is also a universal principle one needs to be aware of. For had Zachariah spoken of his encounter with Gabriel, and the incredible promise delivered, his revelation would have been met with disbelief matching his own and that would prove to be the death of the promise. An idea, particularly one that stretches the imagination to its limits, is a fragile thing. It needs to held closely in one's breast and allowed to gather strength, before it is revealed. And for the same reason, when Elizabeth realized that she was indeed pregnant she hid the fact for five months. One can only imagine the ridicule they both would have been subjected to should the news be spread abroad.

When one does not, or cannot, accept the possibility of a life long dream, a strongly held desire being fulfilled, it is a wise and powerful strategy to remain silent. By not voicing our doubts we allow the concept a chance to grow and gain strength, while the doubts that still lie within us are not open to being confirmed by those with whom we might be tempted to share the concept.

When Gabriel visited Zachariah, the old priest was on duty in the temple; engaged in a ritual he had performed thousands of times over a long lifetime of service. Here we have a living metaphor for that consciousness that is so steeped in tradition and habit that it is rarely open to new possibilities. But lost in the routine of habit his conscious reasoning mind is quiescent, not actively engaged. In this dream-like state, that we all experience from time to time, he is caught unaware when the deep yearning he thought was buried manifests in the appearance of Gabriel (*God is my strength*).

The soul does not miss an opportunity to awaken one to dreams thought impossible, and Zachariah's dream, his heartfelt prayer was that he might father a son, someone who would follow in his footsteps as a man of God. There is a space within his consciousness where this dream has never died.

ZACHARIAH AND ELIZABETH

These two, Zachariah and Elizabeth, were representative of the best within the established religious tradition. "*They were both righteous before God, walking in all the commandments and ordinances of the Lord blameless.*" (Luke 1.6) Together they represent the masculine and feminine energies within the consciousness grown old and caught up in habit, tradition, and appearances, but strong in their faith. They are the union of mind and heart, intellect and soul, out of which is born a bridge from the past to the future, from that which is to that which is to be. They make a good pair, balancing each other in spirit. All of this is necessary for the fulfillment of the promise. It is this consciousness that makes it possible for John to be born.

ELIZABETH AND MARY

The relationship of people in the story is not a matter of chance, but is necessary to the forward movement of the drama. They also serve as important metaphors for our story. Gabriel refers to Elizabeth as a "kinswoman" to Mary, and although it isn't clear how their being related adds any important element to the scriptural account, it is significant to our inner drama. In our inner drama, Mary and Elizabeth each represent an aspect of the feminine nature within the psyche. Mary the rebel, the open-eyed open-hearted adolescent on the verge of womanhood, turns to Elizabeth who is strong in belief and in character; she who has seen something of life, felt some of its pain, and yet carries her own promise. The feminine within each of us, that loving creative life affirming energy, is multidimensional in its expression, and prolific in its creative power. The relationship between Mary and Elizabeth, foretell of a similar relationship between those to whom they give birth.

JOHN THE BAPTIST AND JESUS, THE CHRIST

It is necessary in the story, and in the inner life of man, for the birth of John to precede the birth of Jesus the Christ. John, which means *God is good*, and Jesus, the divine (*I AM*) identity in man, are related in the story, and in man's consciousness.

John, the forerunner of the Christ, is the intellect awakening to its own limitations with the recognition that there is a greater dimension of life to be realized through the rule of spirit. There is a shift that takes place in one's consciousness that is reflected in the words he ultimately speaks as John the Baptist, when referring to the Christ; "He must increase and I must decrease." (John 3.30)

John is the herald, the advance man for the appearance of the Christ. Jesus, the Christ, personified the divine (I Am) dimension in man, the divine connection, to That which Jesus called Father. This is in recognition of the relationship that exists between God and every man/woman. His declaration, "The Father and I are one," describes the intimate nature of that relationship, one that is true for every living soul.

John fulfilled the prophecy of Isaiah regarding "The voice of one crying in the

wilderness; *Make straight the way of the Lord."*
Luke 3.4)   John, as metaphor, fulfills the same
prophecy In the inner life of man as the herald of
the Christ, the evolved spiritual dimension of
man. But the Christ within can only appear when
the intellect, wandering in the wilderness of
doubt, confusion, and disbelief, gives way to the
Light of the Spirit. John the Baptist is vital to the
story, for without the awakened intellect there
can be no birth of the Christ.

And in our world it truly is the voice of one
"crying in the wilderness," for we are all easily
caught up in, and confounded by, the world's
pleasures and treasures. We deny our spiritual
heritage, *made in the image and likeness of
God,* and our true relationship to God. In disbelief we flee from our own truth.

We are like the pursued one in the *Hound
of Heaven,* by Francis Thompson.

> *For though I knew His love who followed,*
> *Yet I was sore adread,*
> *Lest having Him,*
> *I must have naught beside,* (2)

Caught in the snare of our own doubts
and fears, we still wait for the birth of the Christ
within, and dread the price that we fear it may
impose.

44

JOSEPH

In the realm of mind, of consciousness, Joseph's initial response to seek a "quiet divorce" may be better understood when one appreciates that the name Joseph (*Jehovah shall increase*), and refers to that faculty of mind that we know as *imagination*.

When one is asked to *father* a concept that stretches the mind beyond its usual and accepted boundaries, as for instance the belief that each soul is a son/daughter of God, out of fear and disbelief one might well seek a quiet divorce. The idea seems so outrageous, that we can just *imagine* the ridicule it would bring. Our response, like that of Joseph, might be to choose a quiet separation as the best course of action.

And yet it is only our imagination that moves us from one increase to another increase in life. Without it we would still be living in caves huddled around a fire, and communicating in grunts and gestures. Aware of this, Albert Einstein is quoted as saying, "Knowledge is nothing; imagination is everything."

And so Joseph listened to his angelic visitor and took Mary as his wife. The masculine and feminine are joined, as they are in all creative endeavors. But he "knew her not until she had borne a son, and he called his name Jesus." (Matt. 1.25)

There was to be no intimacy, no polluting or altering of the purity of that which was to be born. Only after it is born is its name affirmed. Then it is the father; the masculine left brain energy that names that which is created by the feminine right brain energy. Such is the whole, holy, process of the act of creation.

WHEN ANGELS APPEAR

The entire epic is launched through the activities and assurances of angels. It is the angel Gabriel *(God is my strength)*, who first brought the startling news to the priest Zachariah that his aged and barren wife Elizabeth would conceive and bear a son, and six months later delivered a similar message to Mary. While Joseph, Mary's betrothed, is visited by yet another angel of the Lord, and told not to be afraid to take Mary as his wife, for the child she will bear is of the Holy Spirit. (Note: These details are drawn from the Gospels of Luke, and Matthew, and do not appear in the Gospels of either Mark or John.)

Angel is from the Greek Angelos, which means messenger or messenger of God. They are the bearers of messages, thoughts, ideas, and conceptions direct from God. The messages they convey are never ordinary and this, plus their sudden unexpected appearance, can be frightening. As they did in the story, they will tell us "Do not be afraid." But their messages are so startling, so challenging and unbelievable, that they fly in the face of all reason. The idea or concept lies outside the range of our known world, beyond the realm of our limited experience.

It reaches beyond our self-concept, beyond our belief of who we are, and what we are capable of. It lies outside of our comfort zone and often requires a leap of faith, as it did of Mary, and of Zachariah and Elizabeth, and of Joseph. It is not surprising that our first response grows out of fear.

Remembering the words of the Master that the *kingdom of God is within you*, we should not be surprised that our angels often come from within us, messengers of our Higher Self. Every new idea is like a visit from an angel, a messenger of God, and a manifestation of our higher nature. And, God help us, we habitually dismiss them out of fear and disbelief.

Like Joseph, our first thought is for a quiet divorce, to just separate ourselves from it in a way that does not result in shame or blame, and then who will be the wiser? It will always appear as a singularly frightening threat to the Ego, which believes and wants us to believe that it, like Herod, (who we shall meet later in the story), is "king," the rightful ruler of our world. Our Ego will attempt to avoid by any means the ridicule that any new and radical idea is likely to bring.

And the more glorious the vision, the grander and more radical the idea, the greater is the fear and disbelief. It is entirely true that it is not our failures that we fear the most, it is our glory. And fear it we do for it has its own demands, the greatest of which is that we be willing to change. Heal me we pray, but don't ask me to change.

I know an old man who in his youth was visited by an angel who said, "Hail, O favored one," or something like that, and then proceeded to tell him that he was to go to college and become a journalist, a writer. His response was "How can that be? I have no money for college. I must go to work." The Mary within him was still undiscovered, unknown, and so there was no innocent, receptive feminine presence within him to say "Let it be to me according to your word." The seed found no welcoming womb, and the angel departed and did not return until many years later. Often they do not return at all.

But life is a dynamic process, not a static thing. Genesis is always happening, Spirit is forever declaring, *"Behold! I make all things new"* (Rev. 21.5). If we are aware of that we may, like Joseph, accept the angel's promise as the "fulfillment of a prophecy," a thing foreordained by God, as is our Christ nature. The story of this birth, this life, points to a yet unrealized dimension in us, a way of being in the world, that is divine in nature, and our Mary is to receive and carry it to term.

GABRIEL

Gabriel is an angel of the highest rank, he who *stands in the presence of God*. Considering the awesome nature of the message he brought to Mary, nothing less than the birth of the Christ into the world, God could not choose a lesser emissary. This intimacy with God is the hallmark of that which is to be born, the Christ in man who boldly declares, *The Father and I are one*. The powerful state of consciousness symbolized by the angel Gabriel lives as a potential within each of us. The angel Gabriel is present whenever we *stand in the presence of God*. By taking this stand we center our life and action in the Power and Presence of the living God; *God is our strength*. It is a place where miracles happen.

Following Gabriel's visit, and quickened by the promise of the precious new life in her, Mary sought a place in consciousness of prayer and praise, (Judah). Perhaps the next time we are visited by an angel who brings a message of some incredible possibility in our life, our response might be to *let it be according to your word*. And then we might have the wisdom displayed by Mary, and go to our own place of praise and prayer.

Behold, a virgin shall conceive and bear a son, and his name shall be called Emmanuel! (God with us)

CHAPTER 2

The Birth

The months passed, while the precious new life that Mary carried grew strong, and the time was near for the child to be born. The birth was immanent when a decree went out from Rome, from Caesar Augustus, *"that all the world should be enrolled."* (Luke 2.1) To respond to the imperial order, each individual would have to return to his own city to be registered and counted. Joseph and Mary would have to travel from the city of Nazareth in Galilee, to Bethlehem in Judea, the city of David, because Joseph was of the house and lineage of David.

When Joseph read the decree posted in the town center he wanted to tear it to shreds; Mary could not possibly make such a trip. It was over a hundred miles to Bethlehem and they would have to walk every step of the way, for in her condition Mary could not ride on the back of a plodding donkey. It would take weeks to get there, an endless string of sweltering days and cold nights. It was unthinkable! Impossible! He would not allow it. Nor would he leave her at a time like this, when the birth could take place any day. Joseph found, however, that Mary had other thoughts on the matter.

When Joseph told her of the decree from Rome and expressed his fears for her and the baby, Mary, with the quiet confidence she had shown throughout her pregnancy, told him that nothing was going to happen to this baby. "He will be born when he is ready," she said. Her quiet words were uttered with such firmness, Joseph recognized that further discussion was pointless. He would have to address his concerns in his own time and his own way. There was nothing left to do but to begin making the necessary preparations for the trip.

He was relieved somewhat when he found that several other families from Nazareth, and other parts of Galilee, were to make the same journey. At least they would not be traveling alone; there would be women present should Mary need their special care and attention. The journey was as hard as he had feared, but one would have thought that Mary was on holiday. Exhausted at the end of the day's trek, she greeted each morning with a fresh glow about her as if sustained by some mysterious inner strength that was renewed nightly. It was night-fall when the long journey finally came to an end, and Bethlehem, the city of David, lay before them.

Upon their arrival they found a city over-flowing and overwhelmed. The decree from Rome had brought people from far and wide adding scores to the regular inhabitants. They soon realized that every available lodging space had been taken. Some of the weary travelers huddled together in doorways or at the edge of the surging crowds, while others turned the occasion into a raucous celebration.

Mary was fighting tears of exhaustion when they came at last to an inn where the inn-keeper, although unable to provide lodging within, suggested that they would find space and warmth in the stable behind to the inn. Joseph gratefully accepted the offer, and placing his arm around Mary, led the way to their un-common lodging. He took his cloak, and that of Mary, and made a place of comfort for her on a bed of hay. The place was warmed by the pres-ence of animals and, in contrast to the inn, in the soft light of the lamp it provided a blessed peace and quiet. "And the time came for her to be delivered. And she gave birth to her first-born son and wrapped him in swaddling cloths, and laid him in a manger." (Luke 2.7)

On the outskirts of the city, there were shepherds in the field keeping watch over their flock by night, when suddenly an angel of the Lord appeared. They fell to the ground and hid their faces in fear. But the angel said to them, *"Be not afraid; for behold, I bring you good news of a great joy which will come to all the people; for to you is born this day in the city of David a Savior, who is Christ the Lord."* And the angel gave them a sign to look for; *"you will find a babe wrapped in swaddling cloths and lying in a manger."* (Luke 2.12)

When the vision ended and the angel left, the stunned shepherds looked at each other in amazement, and wondered if what they had seen and heard was real. There was only one way to find out. They drew straws to see who would remain with the flock while the others went to see if what they had been told was true. *"And they went with haste, and found Mary and Joseph, and the babe lying in a manger. And when they saw it, they shared that which they had experienced in the fields, and that which had been told them concerning this child."* (Luke 2.17) And all that heard the shepherd's account wondered about it, but Mary *"kept all these things, pondering them in her heart."* (Luke 2.19)

THE WORD BECOME FLESH

That which was conceived was born; the word became flesh. This Word, this concept, is embedded in the heart of every living soul. It is that Higher Self that is honored everywhere, in every spiritual movement throughout the world, throughout time. It is the Christ of the Christians, the Buddha nature of the Buddhists; the Atman of the Hindus, and if we were to look back through the history of man from the beginning of beginnings, we would find the enlightened soul by other names, at other times and places.

But, in nearly every instance, we make the mistake of turning them into exceptions rather than examples. We see them as divine, for they demonstrate a grasp of things, a view of life that is so clear and complete that we cannot help but see them as such. And divine they are, for the light of the consciousness that they display reveals the divine reality that in inherent in every living soul; each made in the image and likeness of God.

Do these words of Jesus the Christ speak of him as an exception? *"I am the light of the world. He who follows me shall not walk in darkness, but will have the light of life."* (John 8.12) *You are the light of the world."* (Matt. 5.14) *"Take my yoke upon you, and learn from me; for I am gentle and humble in heart, and you will find rest for your souls.* (Matt. 11.29)

His request that we learn from him is asking one to become a disciple, as one would follow a teacher. For this dimension of consciousness to live within, it must first be conceived and carried to its birth in each of us. It must become our story.

Angelus Selesius, the Persian poet, wrote.

> *Christ could be born*
> *a thousand times in Galilee*
> *but all in vain*
> *until He is born in me.* (3)

To live in this conscious oneness is to reveal the Christ within. *"We shall be like him, for we shall see him even as he is."* (1 John 3.2) But only when, this story becomes *our* story, when we recognize, as did the man Jesus, that there is no separation between God and man, that we are one.

It takes a pure heart to find favor in God, to provide the sacred space to carry and nurture such a demanding conception. To do so we need to pray with the Psalmist, *"Create in me a clean heart, O God, and put a new and right spirit within me."* (Ps. 51.10)

But praying alone will not suffice. It is all too easy for us to fall into the same trap as did the Pharisees, those whom Jesus called hypocrites, and of whom Isaiah spoke when he said,

"This people honors me with their lips, but their heart is far from me." (Isaiah 29.13) It seems clear that it will take more than honoring with our lips if we are sincere in seeking this birth within. To prepare a place for the birth we will first have to rid ourselves of a host of things and desires we habitually carry about with us. The Christ cannot become a reality as a veneer, one more thing pasted over our habitual way of being in the world.

But none of this happened in a vacuum. There were forces in the world, as there are in our own psyche, some beneficial and some hostile, some uplifting and others threatening. Such is the case with our story. But how might all this play out as we, like Mary, ponder it in our heart?

CAESAR

Caesar Augustus was Emperor of Rome at the time of the birth of Jesus. It was a time when the Roman Empire covered most of the known world, and ruled it with an iron fist. Caesar Augustus issued a decree requiring that all people falling under the rule of Rome be enrolled, registered and counted.

The name Caesar means sharp, cutting edge, and is symbolic of the reasoning mind, a left-brain way of viewing the world, and Augustus means kingly, venerable. In the realm of mind, of consciousness, this is an archetype of the supremacy of the intellect, of reason. It is the concept of self where reason and will rule with absolute power. It is worldly, temporal power raised to the highest, and it is always plagued by an underlying fear. Not knowing from where the threat may come, it desires (decrees) that *all the world should be enrolled,* identified and accounted for.

When this archetype rules in our consciousness, it does so with the iron fist of will. It is awesome in its power and most dangerous when threatened and, it always feels threatened for it knows the power it exercises is transitory. Its days as supreme ruler are short when the awakened intellect, (John the Baptist), is born in us. It is important to remember however, that as an inner archetype it is not evil. It is simply a way of being in the world through which we all must grow as we learn to, *"Render unto Caesar the things that are Caesar's, and unto God the things that are God's."* (Matt. 22.21)

Joseph rendered unto Caesar when he and Mary went from Galilee to Bethlehem, to the city of David, to be registered. The important symbolism here is that Bethlehem means *house of bread, sustenance,* in the city of David (*Love*). That which was conceived is about to take on form; the Word is to become flesh.

Where they had begun their journey, the village of Nazareth, was a tiny cluster of homes around a single well. It was so commonplace that people scoffed when they heard the name spoken. *"Can any good come out of Nazareth?"* (John 1.46) It was a place that was the perfect symbol for the psychic space necessary for the development of that which now ass born—the Christ.

The Christ nature is not one that is likely to be nurtured in, or emerge from, a place of riches or social position. The Christ can only come from the commonplace; the consciousness caught up in riches and fame is not likely to bring forth the Christ. *"It is easier for a camel to go through the eye of a needle than for a rich man to enter the kingdom of Heaven."* (Luke 18.25)

This is also why there was no room at the inn. Even if there had been space within the inn, it would not have been a suitable place for the birth of this particular child. The symbolic language tells the story more truly. We are looking at two stories here; one is the birth of a boy, and the other is the birth of a new dimension of consciousness, the Christ within each life.

With that in mind, we see that Mary has carried the seed to fullness, while Joseph, (*God shall increase*), has supported the concept. They are summoned by imperial edict to travel to Bethlehem, (*house of bread*), city of David, (*a place of love*). There they find shelter in a stable, a shelter for animals, where the child is laid in a manger, a place of sustenance. That which was conceived had to come from a place of love and take on substance (flesh), the first expression of which for humankind is the animal nature. The child was wrapped in swaddling cloths, symbolic of the confinement of spirit in flesh.

"In the beginning was the Word, and the word was with God, and the word was God, and the word became flesh and dwelt among us." (John 1.1) Every living soul is the Word become flesh, each carrying the seed of the Christ.

All creation moves from the invisible to the visible. Everything created is first fashioned in the invisible word, image, or concept. To have existence in form, that invisible concept must first be accepted and nurtured in a suitable womb. For a seed, it is the earth; for an idea, it is the mind and heart, and for a child it is in the womb of a woman.

When Mary gave birth to Jesus, she gave birth to the concept of the perfected man, he whose birth the angels had heralded and the prophets foretold. It was a prophecy that had not gone unnoticed. As with all high drama, there were dangerous forces arrayed against our hero. For there were those in the world, as there are in our inner drama, that see the divine child as a threat, and wish to eliminate him. (Matt. 2.1)

CHAPTER 3

The Wise Men and Herod

When Jesus was born in Bethlehem, in Judea, it was during the reign of Herod, a name that means hero-born or heroic, but there was little about him that was heroic. He thought of himself, and was addressed as, "king of the Jews" but he was not a king. He was governor of the area, one of a series appointed by Rome, who served at the pleasure and whim of Caesar. He was a vicious, brutal, paranoid who would kill anyone he thought posed a threat to his rule, and that included members of his own family, a number of whom he had killed.

One can easily imagine his response when word reached him of three richly dressed strangers in the province, identified as *"wise men from the east,"* who were asking, *"Where is he that is born king of the Jews? "* (Matt. 2-1) They had seen a star in the eastern sky that foretold of the birth, and had come to worship the child. Herod

61

was barely able to mask his fear and rage at the audacity of the question. Strangers or not, did they not know that he, and he alone, was king of the Jews? His first impulse was to have the strangers immediately seized and killed, slowly and painfully while they learned who really was the king of the Jews. But like all tyrants, his cruelty was matched only by his cunning, and he was prepared to find a way to use the strangers and their mission.

He assembled all the chief priests and scribes of the people and asked them where the Christ was to be born. (Matt. 2.4) They told him that according to the prophecy the birth would take place in Bethlehem. With that information Herod summoned the wise men secretly and, with a great show of interest and wonder, asked them about the star, and what time it had appeared. When they told him, he shared with them the prophecy that pointed to Bethlehem as the location of the birth. Then Herod, with a smile on his face that masked the fear in his heart, asked that they *"Go and search diligently for the child, and when you have found him bring me word, that I too may come and worship him."* (Matt. 2.8)

But the wise men, being truly wise, saw through Herod's transparent effort to use them in this way. After their audience with Herod, they went on their way, *"and the star they had*

*seen in the East went before them, until it came to
rest over the place where the child was. And
when they entered the dwelling place they saw
the child with Mary his mother, and they fell
down and worshipped him."* (Matt. 2.11) Then,
opening their treasures, they offered the child
gifts of gold, and frankincense, and myrrh.
Their mission complete, the wise men were
*"warned in a dream not to return to Herod, and
they departed to their own country by another
way."* (Matt. 2.12)

HEROD

Herod is no stranger to us. In one form or
another he still struts about in the world, and we
have seen him reflected in every tyrant who has
ever lived. They have often appeared as heroic
to their followers, but their reign is always one of
brute force and terror and they are quick to
eliminate any threat, real or imagined.

In our inner life Herod represents the Ego,
which like Herod believes that it is "king," sover-
eign in our life, and our world. For a time, often
years, we accept that as the truth of our total
being; the Ego and I are one is our truth. Under
its rule we are constantly engaged, sometimes
heroically, in proving how worthy we are of respect and love. But, like Herod, the Ego never sits
securely on its throne and is easily "troubled,"
fearful of any threat to its rule. Ultimately word

reaches the Ego, as it did Herod, that there are "Wise men" from the East, (in metaphysical terms *from within*), who have seen a sign in the heavens that told of the birth of one who was to be king—the Christ. But the Ego, like Herod, will act quickly to eliminate any threat to its rule.

This struggle between the Ego and the Christ, between the temporal and the spiritual, is between fear and love. *"Every thought you have is either a thought of love or of fear."* (A *Course in Miracles*, Workbook p. 26) Love is the essence of the Christ consciousness, while fear is the dominant emotion that drives the Ego, as it did Herod. The Ego's fear of being replaced by Christ is the same as that of Herod; survival is uppermost in the life of each.

We will not find it necessary, however, to kill the Ego for the Christ to survive and thrive. With the passage time, and the natural process of growth under the influence of the Christ, the Ego will "ripen" into a more developed and healthy version of itself, as the more benign Archelaus, *(people's chief)* came to replace Herod as provincial ruler. But, who are the Wise Men and what are they doing in our story?

THE WISE MEN

The wise men were seers, magi, astrologers and the interpreters of dreams, those to whom temporal rulers turned for counsel. They studied the heavens, both the night skies and the celestial realm of consciousness. They held great power and possessed the richest of gifts, and they came from the East.

Their appearance and their mission certainly "troubled" Herod, as they trouble the Ego. They possess and radiate a unique power that is not based upon worldly wealth, status, or position. They are strangers to Herod, and to the Ego.

Herod attempts to manipulate them, to make them unwitting allies in locating the threat. They possess a key to the location, for they have seen a star in the heavens, in the East (within), and have followed it.

As astrologers they have seen a pattern in the heavens that foretell of the birth of a ruler. The star which they see, like the morning star, points to a new dawn in the affairs of man, as it heralds the coming of the light and the glory of the sun—the Son. It represents the awakening to the Christ, the Son of the Most High, and the dawn of a new consciousness for *all* people. The promise was, *"I bring you good news of a great joy which will come to all the people."* (Luke 2.10) The Christ presence, the Christ consciousness, is not confined to any one group people, or religion, or spiritual path. The Christ mind, or consciousness, is a universal promise and potential born in the heart of every living soul.

The wise men brought precious gifts of gold, frankincense and myrrh. In our inner drama, the wise men from the East, from within us, offer the holy child, the Christ within, precious gifts. The gifts symbolize qualities and characteristics of the consciousness of the holy child, of that which has been born. They are spiritual gifts and powers.

Gold represents spiritual riches. The ancient alchemists searched endlessly for the secret by which they might turn lead into gold, a base metal into a precious one. There could not be a more appropriate metaphor, or symbol, for the spiritual process of turning the base human, the one caught up entirely in the senses, into the divine god-man, the Christ within.

Frankincense and Myrrh are both aromatic gum resins, used as incense and in medicine. Incense is often used to create a sense of sacred space, an invitation to the holy. When Zachariah was visited by Gabriel, it had had been during hour of the incense. These resin gums were also used for medicinal purposes, and are symbolic of the gift of spiritual healing.

CHAPTER 4

The Flight into Egypt, and Return

When the Wise Men had departed, an angel of the Lord appeared to Joseph in a dream, and warned him that the child was in mortal danger. He was to take the child and his mother, and flee to Egypt, for Herod was about to institute a search for the child, to destroy him. (Matt. 2.13) Heeding the warning, Joseph took the child and his mother that very night and departed to Egypt, where they remained beyond Herod's reach and rage. And terrible was that rage.

When Herod realized that his attempt to use the Wise Men in their search for the child had failed, he flew into a vicious rage. He ordered that all male children, two years old or under in Bethlehem, and the entire region, were to be killed.

Joseph and Mary and the child remained in Egypt until Joseph had yet another dream. An angel of the Lord appeared to Joseph in a dream, and told him that it was safe to take the child and Mary and return to Israel, *"for those who sought the child's life are dead."* (Matt. 2.20) And so they returned to Israel.

But the threat to the child was not entirely removed with the death of Herod, for Archelaus is Herod's son, and as the saying goes, the fruit doesn't fall very far from the tree. Archelaus must have been a very clever son to grow to manhood in the house of the paranoid Herod. And it was true that he brought a more tolerant nature to the governing of the region, but it would have been foolish for anyone to assume that he would be any more benign than Herod toward one who was born to be "king of the Jews."

Aware of this, Joseph was still concerned for the life of the child and settled his family in the town of Nazareth, in Galilee. Here was a place so common, so little thought of, that no one was likely to believe it could harbor any person of significance. For the next three decades Joseph and his family lived there while the Christ child grew to manhood.

EGYPT AND THE PHARAOH

When Joseph took Mary and the Christ child to Egypt, he had physically removed the child from the reach of Herod, a move that would allow the new- born to grow in safety. But viewed as a metaphor the move speaks with greater depth of meaning, for the move is as critical to the survival of the idea of the Christ in you, as it was to the safety of the boy Jesus. One is removed from the threat of Herod, the other from the threat of the rational mind, ruled by the Ego. Both must flee to Egypt for safety.

Egypt was ruled by the Pharaoh, earthly incarnation of Ra, the Sun God. As a symbol it refers to that brain and nerve center which we call the Solar Plexus, the seat of the autonomic nervous system. It is that mysterious and little understood realm of substance and life in the depths of the body consciousness that regulates the unconscious activities of the body. It breathes us, and beats our heart, and marshals the resources needed to meet threats to the body wellness. It is the realm of our nocturnal dreams, and the womb of creation within us.

It is here that the child, the tiny vulnerable new born baby (or concept), can be held safe from the doubting, questioning, even lethal, ra- tional mind, the natural realm of the Ego (Herod). It is also the region of intuition, of "gut feeling." It is the sacred space where we entertain angels of the Lord, where we contact and commune with our higher, God Self. For *"Behold, the kingdom of God is in the midst of you."* (Luke 17.21) It is here that the tiny Christ child can grow in safety, as must any new concept, away from those forces that would, out of fear and ignorance, kill it.

When Joseph learned of Herod's death, the Christ child now strong enough, they returned to Nazareth where the child grew *"in wisdom and stature, and in favor with God and man."* (Luke 2.52) When the ego no longer functions as the supreme ruler of one's mind, one's life, then the Christ idea, the Christ consciousness, can grow and mature along with a more healthy and enlightened ego.

His name and nature, his way of being in the world, shall be called Immanuel, *(God is with us)*. Christ is more than the title given one illumined man, it is the personification, the actualization of the *(I AM)* spiritual identity that resides in every soul. But the story thus far tells us only of the birth and early nurturing of the concept, the Christ child. There is much more to be told. What is to happen to our young hero, and how will those events serve as metaphor to a broader deeper meaning of the life exemplified?

With how much of this drama do you identify? It is painfully apparent that the Ego (Herod) continues to rule in our lives much of the time, while the Christ within may still be a stranger to us, or at best a nodding acquaintance, but don't despair. As you consider how torturously slow we grow in spiritual awareness, remember his words to his disciples when they were frightened out of their minds by the storm. *"Take heart, it is I; have no fear."* (Mark 6.50)

There is within you, and me, and every living soul, the Higher Self, the Christ. The only question is, where along the path do we find ourselves? It will help for us to recognize that none of the characters in the story are villains. The joyful truth is that like their reflections that live within each of us, they are all our teachers.

So we have the story thus far. The magnificent conception is nurtured and carried to its birth; the Word is become flesh. We can see that it is not an easy process, for there is danger of annihilation at every turn. But it is the natural way of things, a movement from the invisible to the visible, from the formless to the form, from non-existence to existence, only to return again to the Void, that great ocean of infinite potential that we find in Genesis.

With the conception and birth of the Christ consciousness, we have picked up our story in the middle. Our journey really began with the creation of man, with the Adam consciousness. But God, the Self-existent One, was at work in the timeless time before that, in the beginning of beginnings, in Genesis.

Be not afraid; for behold, I bring you good news of a great joy which will come to all the people.

PART II

IN THE BEGINNING

What is man, that thou dost make so much of him, and that thou dost set thy mind upon him, thou dost visit him every morning, and test him every moment? (Job 7.17)

This is the story of our ancestor Adam, the first man/woman to appear out of the creative activity of God. He came last in the sequence of events but filled a special place in the Mind of God, for he was *"made in the image and likeness of God,"* (Gen. 1-27) a Son of the Most High. Actually he was next to the last of God's creations, a creation that would have been incomplete without Eve, Adam's other half and the mother of all humankind.

They were born into an existence of utter bliss, the Garden of Eden, but it was not within God's plans, or man's nature, for them to remain there. God was not entirely finished with his creation. Adam and Eve in their blissful existence were unconscious of their true nature, and completely unaware that they were made in God's image and likeness. They were blissfully ignorant or ignorantly blissful and this could not continue; this was not to be their destiny. Their destiny lay in the fully awakened consciousness of the Christ, that state of mind and heart that in full awareness could boldly declare, "The Father and I are one." So God contrived a clever plot.

For five days God labored mightily, and from his initial creation of heaven and earth, brought forth Light and darkness, day and night, the Sun, Moon, stars and planets, the seas and dry land, and vegetation of all kinds. He fashioned mountains and valleys, streams and rivers, and then....

CHAPTER 5

God Created Man — Twice

Spiritual Man

"*God created man in his own image, in the image and likeness of God he created him; male and female he created them.*" (Gen. 1.27)

Man of Earth

Then the Lord God "*formed man of the dust of the ground, and breathed into his nostrils the breath of life; and man became a living being.*" (Gen. 2.7)

THE TWOFOLD NATURE OF MAN

Our story begins with God having created man twice; first in His own "*image and likeness,*" and then out of the "*dust of the earth.*" The first is the essential spiritual nature of man/woman, the divine dimension in every living soul. God blessed them, and said to them, "Be fruitful and multiply, and fill the earth and subdue it." With this, God had finished his work, for it was the sixth day. *"And God saw everything that he had made, and behold, it was very good."* (Gen. 1.28 – 31)

It turned out, however, that God was not quite finished. It was true that he had created spiritual man/woman in his image and likeness, but a purely spiritual being was not equipped to deal physically with the earth. He realized that *"there was no man to till the ground."* (Gen. 2.5) With this realization, the *"Lord God formed man of dust from the ground, and breathed into his nostrils the breath of life; and man became a living being."* (Gen. 2.7)

That which was divine, made in the image and likeness of God, was given substance. The Word became flesh and was now subject to all the joys and pains of this new dimension of being. This points to a basic truth about the essential nature of man, a dual nature, for we are both human and divine. One without the other is incomplete, and foolish indeed is the person who calls the one good and the other evil.

God Planted a Garden in Eden

God planted a garden, "in Eden, in the East," and there he put man. In that garden, God made to grow "every tree that is pleasant to the sight and good for food, the tree of life is also in the midst of the garden, and the tree of the knowledge of good and evil." (Gen. 2.8 – 9)

THE GARDEN

Eden in Hebrew means pleasure or delight, and points to that blissful state of being that one might experience when all things are provided, all needs fulfilled, without any thought, worry or struggle. This blissful state of being is like that of a tiny child whose every care is met, and who does not yet see himself as separate from the world that surrounds him. This is the Adam consciousness into which we are each born. But it does not, can not, last; God had other plans for Adam.

God did not intend that man, made in his image and likeness, a creative center of life itself, was to simply lie around drinking ambrosia and eating the fruits of this lush garden. The "*garden*" is a metaphor for life itself, the very "*ground*" that God intended that man should till.

This Garden, a place of limitless potential, needs someone to cultivate it, to nurture and care for it, to enrich it. It is located *East of Eden* and, in the world of metaphysical thought and contemplation *East* is located *within*, in the inner reaches of man's being. In the midst of this garden, a wonderful metaphor for life itself, there grows trees that are a delight to see, and good for food. Also growing there is the tree of life eternal, and the tree of the knowledge of good and evil." (Gen. 2.9) That which was pure Spirit is now clothed in flesh, and man has become *a living being.*

This *"garden"* is that place that God had in mind when he realized that someone was needed to *"till the ground."* It is a place that offers infinite possibilities as to what may be planted, and grown, but the ground must be cultivated, as one tends and cultivates one's mind, one's consciousness, one's life, as a place of infinite possibilities. It was, however, a work in progress for God who realized that something was missing.

A Helper for Adam

The Lord God observed that it was *"not good that the man should be alone,"* and decided to *"make him a helper fit for him."* (Gen. 2.18) So out of the ground the Lord God formed every beast of the field and every bird of the air, in an effort to find an appropriate helper for man. He brought them to the man to see what he would call them; and whatever the man called every living creature, that was its name.

THE POWER TO NAME

Adam, this pristine consciousness, was faced with a myriad of sights and sounds, tastes and feelings, when all the creatures of the waters and of the earth, all the life forms were brought before him to see what he would call them. And whatever he called them, that was their name.

This God-like creative power to name a thing is given only to man, s/he who is made in the image and likeness of God. This is the same power that is contained in the words used by God to create everything. "And God said, let there be"— and there was.

This speaking of the word, the naming of anything, is the essential power to create that is vested in man; it is man saying, Let there be. The act of naming a thing not only attaches to the thing an identity but, in a larger sense, gives birth to it. Whatever we name it, that is its name, and the name contains, reflects, the nature of the thing as we see it. Shakespeare wrote, "What's in a name?" For man, it is his whole world, for out of this power to name, we create our world, that private, personal world of consciousness in which we live, and move, and have our being.

Our personal world is the product of our perception of the world. It is both how we see and how we interpret the flow of life around us — people, events, and circumstances that we en-counter and experience. And out of our seeing and interpreting, an activity which is highly sub-jective, we name all of it. The result is highly subjective because our first question is always some form of, Is this for us or against us, supporting or threatening, pleasurable or painful, good or evil?

The power to name the things, situations and circumstances of our life, is a useful power to possess. Without the capacity to label a thing we would live in an overwhelming jumble of impressions and stimuli, but there is a hazard, and a loss in the exercise of it. In the act, the habit, of naming the people, events, and circumstances that enter *our* world we miss the *is-ness* of that which is before us. When that occurs, and it happens quite unconsciously, the label takes on so much power that it stands in the way of our seeing the reality of the moment.

Words, names, labels, are wonderful tools of the mind, and powerful creative agents when fueled by feeling, conviction. It is easy to be seduced into believing that they are the thing itself. They should probably be marked "Danger! Handle with care!" They are, as Adam discovered, powerful creative agents.

In the beginning was the Word, the name, and God said, "*Let there be Light, and there was Light.*" We display the same power in *our* world every time we give name anything. The name, the word, is the seed we plant in our garden, and the name we choose is based on our perception of the thing in relation to our concept of ourselves. How careful we are in choosing the word, the seed we plant, determines the health and beauty of our garden — the quality of our life.

Such is the power of the word. *"It is not what goes into the mouth that defiles a person, but it is what comes out of the mouth that defiles."* (Mark 7.15)

God Created Eve

Though Adam named all the creatures, all living things, not one was found to be a helper fit for him. *"Then the Lord God caused a deep sleep to fall upon Adam, and while he slept the Lord God took one of his ribs which he made into a woman and brought her to the man."* Then the man said, *"This at last is bone of my bones and flesh of my flesh; she shall be called Woman, because she was taken out of Man."*

THE OTHER HALF

The only helper fit for man was woman, the other half of man's being. She could not have been brought forth in any other way except *"out of Man."* She had been there since the beginning, for when God created man in his image and likeness he created *them* *"male and female."* And since man was made in God's image and likeness it is clear that within the Wholeness of God there was/is the duality of the masculine and the feminine. This dual nature is repeated throughout all of creation.

81

In the beginning God did not *create* the heavens and the earth they were always there within the Wholeness of God. Out of the pairing of Heaven and Earth there came Light and darkness, followed by an infinite flow of *apparent* opposites. It is this interplay of opposites that gives rise to all creation.

Lao Tzu, a Chinese philosopher, sixth century B.C., called this interplay of opposites the Tao, which means *The Way*. He is the reputed author of the *Tao Te Ching*, a book of a few thousand words that is the basis for Chinese classical philosophy. In that book we find these opening words.

The Beginning of Power

The Tao that can be expressed
Is not the Tao of the Absolute.
The name that can be named
Is not the name of the Absolute.
The nameless originated Heaven and Earth
The named is the Mother of All Things.
Translation by R. L. Wing (4)

This is the world of duality that we habitually see and, although useful, it is a limited seeing. A little thought reveals that they are *opposite* ends of the same stick, that one cannot exist without the other, and thus they form a whole.

82

Nothing symbolizes this interplay quite so beauti-fully and powerfully as the Taoist symbol of the Yin and Yang. Here we have two fish-like figures, one flowing inevitably into the other, while each contains a piece of the other, and all is held within a circle, the oldest symbol for God, never beginning and never ending.

Fig. 1

The truth is that Adam, Man, is incomplete without Woman. Two halves of a whole, they complete each other. Only she can be a fit helper, for only then can they, like the rest of creation, fit together in a way to produce after their kind. So when people ask about your "bet-ter half," the jest is wrapped in truth, at least concerning your *other* half. And no life is com-plete, or balanced, without the feminine and masculine each being recognized and nourished within the individual. There is a lack, a critical imbalance—spiritually, mentally, and emotionally —in a life that has not honored and developed these two complementary energies, which Carl Jung called the Animus and Anima.

Once again we see the beauty and wisdom of the Taoist symbol, wherein each half contains some of the other. Adam recognized this, for when God brought the woman to him, Adam said, "This at last is bone of my bones and flesh of my flesh." (Gen. 2.23) And the man and woman were both naked and were not ashamed, but that is about to change.

When the Lord God placed man in the garden to till it and keep it, he told him that he could freely eat of every tree of the garden except for the tree of the knowledge of good and evil. His warning was, "*in the day that you eat of it you shall die.*"

This tree was in the midst of the garden, and the garden is in the midst of the life that is man. At first blush it looks as though God is playing the game, *Gotcha!* But remember, "*God saw everything that he had made, and behold, it was very good.*" (Gen. 1.31) The stage is now set for the fall of Adam, of man—a fall upward.

CHAPTER 6

The Fall of Adam —
a Fall Upward

The serpent now entered the story, a creature more wily and subtle than any other that God had created. He asked the woman if God had told her that they were not to eat the fruit of any tree of the garden, and she replied, *"We may eat of the fruit of the trees of the garden; but God said, 'You shall not eat of the fruit of the tree which is in the midst of the garden, neither shall you touch it, lest you die.'"* But the serpent said to the woman, *"You will not die, for God knows that when you eat of it your eyes will be opened, and you will be like God, knowing good and evil."* (Gen. 3.1-5)

When the woman saw that the tree was good for food, and a delight to the eyes, and that it would make one *"be like God, she took of its fruit and ate; and she also gave some to her husband, and he ate. Then the eyes of both were opened, and they knew that they were naked; and they sewed fig leaves together and made themselves loincloths"*..

THE SERPENT

The serpent, a creature that often appears in mythology, is here presented as the villain. But is it? God placed a tree in "the midst of the garden," a tree that was a "delight to the eyes," and the fruit was not only "good to eat," but would also "make one wise." Who could long resist such a temptation? But nothing superfluous is contained within this sacred story, nothing that does not specifically add materially to the whole.

Consider the thought that every garden has its serpent. In a creation structured on the interplay of opposites, you cannot have paradise won without paradise lost. The serpent is an archetypal figure that appears throughout the ages in religion and mythology.

The serpent is a symbol of wisdom and healing; it appears entwined on the staff of Caduceus, the symbol of physicians. The coiled serpent is a symbol of energy awaiting release. Hindu ritual and practice of Kundalini envisions spiritual energy (*prana*), coiled like a serpent at the base of the spine, in an energy center called the "root" chakra. The nature of the energy focused here is primal, sexual, in nature. When raised through spiritual practice to the crown chakra, the central point at the top of the head, it is transformed into the highest expression of spiritual awareness.

But in its primal state as in Adam and Eve, it is sensual, instinctual. It is the seat of desire that leads to a physical joining of man with woman, without which man could not, as do all other creatures, produce "after their kind." Whatever its nature, in the story of Genesis it is an agent of change, a change that is inevitable.

At the serpent's prompting, Eve ate the fruit of the tree of the knowledge of good and evil, as did Adam, and "the eyes of both were opened," (Gen. 3.7) and in that instant they crossed the threshold from essential being to existential being, from simple awareness to self-awareness. It was a shift from a sense of being one with God, one with all of creation, to a perception of being separate from God and from all of God's creation. The moment an awareness of self occurs, everyone and everything else is not-self, and out of this sense of separateness there is born the belief of good and evil.

This misconception, this belief in being separate from God, from our fellow man, from all of creation, is the only thing that may rightly be called original sin. It is in this moment that Satan is born, for every form of evil in the world is spawned from this erroneous belief. It is here that ignorance is born, that fear is born, and all the horrors they give birth to.

This threshold in consciousness is a universal experience of all mankind. Every child in his/her growth in consciousness crosses over this point of consciousness from a sense of oneness with their world, a world in which they see even their toys as being alive, to a sense of separateness. It is this crossing over that makes humankind unique among God's creatures, but it does not come without a price. The price is set forth here in the judgment that God imposes on each of the players in the drama when he learns of their actions.

The Judgments of God:

Adam heard God walking in the garden and was afraid when the Lord God called to him, for he realized that he was naked. Then God asked two questions to which he must already have known the answer; *"Who told you that you were naked? Have you eaten of the tree of which I commanded you not to eat?"* (Gen. 3.11)

In Adam's response we have the first incidence of buck-passing, or the Devil made me do it explanation. He blames Eve, saying, *"The woman whom thou gave to be with me, she gave me fruit of the tree, and I ate."* And when God asked Eve, *"What is this that you have done?"* She replied, *"The serpent beguiled me, and I ate."*

(Gen. 3.12) The serpent has no one to blame, except perhaps God, for setting the whole thing in motion. It was a tactic that did not save any of them from the consequence of their actions, and each was *"cursed"* by God.

The Curse on the Serpent

The serpent was cursed *"above all cattle, and above all wild animals"* to crawl upon his belly, and to eat dust all the days of his life. And God added, *"I will put enmity between you and the woman, and between your seed and her seed; he shall bruise your head, and you shall strike his heel."* (Gen. 3.14)

The Curse on the Woman

The curse upon the woman was that God would *"greatly multiply her pain in childbearing; and yet her desire shall be for her husband, who will rule over her."* (Gen. 3.16)

The Curse on Adam

God's curse upon Adam, because he had listened to Eve, was, *"cursed is the ground because of you; in toil you shall eat of it all the days of your life; thorns and thistles it shall bring forth to you; and you shall eat the plants of the field. In the sweat of your face you shall eat bread till you return to the ground, for out of it you were taken; you are dust, and to dust you shall return."* (Gen. 17 – 19)

THE WAY OF ALL FLESH

Every living creature, all *forms* of life, return to the dust to the earth from which they have come. This is not the earth as we think of it. It is that *earth* that is the unformed substance of God, that ocean of intelligence and energy that was in the beginning, is now, and ever shall be. It is that aspect of Spirit that is ever forming into new creations. *"Behold! I make all things new."* (Rev. 21.5)

The spiritual man, s/he who is made in the image and likeness of God, shall never die. God is the great creative force, the great Experiencer, while man is a microcosm of that creative force which, by its very nature, is continually creating —becoming.

Genesis is a forever happening; It is always *in the beginning.* And man, because of this legacy, is granted *dominion,* a power that has been mistakenly thought of as meaning *to dominate.* This narrow and ignorant view is born out of man's sense of separation from God, from his fellow man, and from the world at large. Until we recognize this lack in our spiritual sight, we will continue to blindly inflict injury on each other and on the earth itself.

It would appear from the story that God created man with the freedom to choose, and the propensity for making what appeared to be the wrong choice, and then got angry at the result. But the story would be incomplete if Adam and Eve had remained in the garden, for it would not be true to the nature of man/woman, and to what lay before them. Once their eyes were opened, once their awareness crossed that threshold of consciousness, from essential being to existential being, nothing would ever look the same again, or be perceived in the same way.

The judgment of God was a life sentence imposed on each, but rather than a curse it was simply a consequence that flows from the essential nature of each. The natural consequence of their awakening consciousness was that they be expelled from the garden, but it was the awakening that served to expel them rather than the anger of God.

Then the Lord God made "*garments of skins*" to clothe Adam and Eve. (Gen. 3.21) This could be read as his having clothed them in the skins of animals, but it doesn't say that. It is more likely that Adam and Eve had become aware of their own skin, that boundary which we perceive separates us from our environment, from each other, and from the world at large.

Once again our perception leads us astray. Our skin, the largest organ of our body, is that living membrane which *connects* us to our physical environment, to each other, and to all of life. This misperception is the cause of much grief in our interaction with our fellow man, and with the world at large.

A FEARFUL GOD?

Then the Lord God said, "*Behold, the man has become like one of us, knowing good and evil,*" and then expressed his fear that man might now "*eat of the tree of life, and live forever.*" (Gen. 3.22) But wait, didn't God see "*everything that he had made, and behold, it was very good.*" (Gen. 1.31) Where then did evil come from, other than from man's misperception? And man, in his spiritual being, is *already* like God, "*in the image and likeness of God he made them; male and female he made them.*" (Gen. 1.27)

So it is the man of earth, of the dust, that is condemned to die. It is man's body that returns to the earth; the man of Spirit is eternal and the experience that we call death is truly a new birth, s/he simply discards one body in order to don another.

Expelled From the Garden

"Therefore, the Lord God sent him forth from the Garden of Eden to till the ground from which he was taken. He drove out the man; and at the East of the Garden of Eden he placed the cherubim, and a flaming sword that turned every way, to guard the way to the tree of life."
(Gen. 3.23)

DRIVEN OUT

The Garden of Eden is a sacred space in consciousness where a sense of oneness with God, and of the essential goodness and rightness, the unity of all creation, is experienced. It is a state of bliss. But as long as we continue to be caught up in the experience of the fruits of the tree of good and evil, the garden will elude us.

When Adam and Eve awakened and were expelled from the Garden of Eden they set mankind upon the mythical hero's journey, the quest for the Holy Grail. It is a desire that lies like a firebrand in the heart of mankind, this yearning to return to the garden, and to a reunion with God. The difference is that this is to be a *conscious* reunion.

It is to experience in the existential being that which was lost when the essential being was left behind in the garden. All the spiritual paths devised by man have this one objective in mind.

It is the *natural mind* of the Taoists, the *clear unattached mind* of the Buddhists; it is the *Christ mind* of the Christians, and the *beginner's mind* of Zen. It is called by various names like *enlightenment, salvation, liberation, satori, nirvana, bliss,* and a host of others. There are many paths, with but one goal, all leading to the same sacred space.

The space is guarded by "*a flaming sword, which turned every way to guard the way to the tree of life.*" (Gen. 3.24)

The flaming sword is a symbol for Truth that man **is** made in the image and likeness of God, *I AM THAT I AM.* (Ex. 3.14) And for man to return to the garden, which like heaven is *within* him, he must ultimately throw himself on the point of that sword and let it pierce his heart. He must come to recognize and declare, as did the man Jesus, the Christ, "*I Am the Life, the Truth, and the Way.*"

PART III

THE FATEFUL JOURNEY

Here is Christ as the Great Example for all mankind, rather than the Great Exception. "I am come that they might have life, and have it more abundantly."

The story of the life of Jesus is the story of man/woman evolving into the Christ. It is a story of great promise, one that provides us with a perfect and powerful example, of how we might live more fully, more abundantly, by discovering the Christ within.

Repent!
The kingdom of heaven is at hand ...
for the kingdom of God is in the
midst of you.

CHAPTER 7

The Road to Jerusalem

He was on his way to Jerusalem (*place of peace*), but he knew there would be no peace for him on this journey. It was the feast of Passover, and he was a young rabbi, a teacher who preached a new religion, healed the sick, attracted a following, and in the process had angered the established religious authorities. He was swept up in a tide of events that seemed to leave him as little choice as a stone in flight. Where had it all begun? Lulled by the gentle rhythmic movement of the small beast under him, the memory of that fateful day on the banks of the river Jordan filled his mind.

The Baptism of Jesus

His kinsman, John, stood waist-deep in the river flow, his strong arms lifted heavenward, and in a voice like rolling thunder his cry poured into the heavens and over the large crowd standing on the banks. *"Repent, for the kingdom of heaven is at hand."* (Luke 3.1) Known as John the Baptist, his warning cry was seen as the fulfillment of the words of the prophet Isaiah, *"The voice of one crying out in the wilderness; Prepare the way of the Lord, make his paths straight."* (Matt. 2.3)

He was a strange and wonderful sight to behold, clad in a rough garment of camel's hair cinched at the waist with a leather belt, his long hair tossed wildly in the wind. There was a fierce magnetism about him, an elemental force like the wind itself. But it was his eyes that caught and held you, that seemed to see through to your very soul, and his voice like the lash of a whip that stung you repeatedly until you heeded his call, and repented your sins, and were baptized.

Jesus stood at the edge of the crowd. He had the same lean look as John, and nearly as tall. he could see over the heads of most of those gathered. In contrast to John, an aura of quiet power and serenity radiated from him that was felt by those standing nearby. The curious glances and whispered comments rippled out over the crowd in ever-widening circles. He took no notice; his attention was on John.

He had not seen John since they played together as children, and was surprised at the size of the gathering. It even included a sprinkling of Pharisees and Sadducees, the religiously educated keepers and interpreters of the law. Their concern was always with the letter of the law rather than the spirit. John addressed them scornfully as a "brood of vipers," and challenged them to bear fruit worthy of repentance.

It was at that moment that Jesus had made his way to the water's edge and called out to John, *"Baptize me."* John's piercing eyes widened with surprise, and his face and his voice softened, as he said, *"I need to be baptized by you, and yet you come to me?"* Jesus, who now stood next to him in the water, said, *"Let it be so now; for it is proper for us in this way to fulfill all righteousness."* And so John baptized him.

When Jesus arose from the water he had a vision of the heavens opening, and the Spirit of God descending like a dove that hovered above his head. And he heard a voice saying, *"This is my beloved Son with whom I am well pleased."* (Luke 3.17)

All the days of his thirty years on earth, days filled with the thoughts, the questions, the searching, the study, the contemplation, all fused together and were sanctified in that holy instant. He was alive with the Holy Spirit, filled with an awesome power and ecstasy that left him breathless. He felt the need to be alone, to consider what it was that had just happened to him, and was *"led by the Spirit into the wilderness," where he "fasted forty days and forty nights."* (Matt. 4.1)

A DESTINED MEETING

This meeting between Jesus and John the Baptist was foreordained, etched into the destiny of each at their birth, as it is in the inner life of man. It was as inevitable in the course of their lives, as it is in the fulfillment of what they represent in the evolving consciousness of man, where they exist as archetypal energies, potential ways of being in the world, for every living soul. As metaphor they represent the awakened, aspiring, intellect (John the Baptist), recognizing and blessing the spiritually evolved man (the Christ).

John, the awakening intellect has become aware of a profound lack in a life that is lived wholly on the surface, a life that is engaged in the incessant attempt to find meaning through the satisfaction of the urging of the five senses. Such a life is one where each new acquisition, each new thrill, is short-lived and leaves one with a recurring emptiness that cannot be filled with the things of this world.

Out of this deep gnawing sense that something vital is missing, a hunger grows, and with it a question. Is that all there is? When the pain is sufficient, and the question will not leave one alone, an urge rises from deep within the soul that sets one on the path in search of the Holy Grail. And from the depths one hears the whispered cry, "*Repent! The kingdom of heaven is at hand.*"

When John baptized Jesus, it was symbolic of the intellect acknowledging the superiority of Spirit. It was the mind acknowledging the rulership of the heart with the words, "*I need to be baptized by you, and do you come to me?*" And Spirit's response, "*Let is be so for now; for thus it is fitting for us to fulfill all righteousness.*"

It is right that this be so, for the encounter is not one in which there is a winner and a loser, one triumphant and the other defeated and displaced. Both are enhanced and both are needed to insure the wholeness of the individual life and evolving consciousness. The encounter is Holy.

The mind without the heart is cold, while the heart without the mind tends to be mushy sentimentality, and either one alone is incomplete. In these we again have the eternal pairs that appear throughout scripture—heaven and earth, light and darkness, male and female, yang and yin, mind and heart. They are not opposites but complementary. In their union there is wholeness, and wisdom.

John, the awakened intellect, stands in the midst of the flow of the river of life, of consciousness. This is that state of mind that has recognized the transient nature of the things of the world, their ultimate emptiness and distracting power, and has renounced them. He stands as a symbol of the *natural* man, clothed in the skins of animals and eating only locusts and honey. He is a soul driven by one ambition only, and that is to "*Prepare the way of the Lord, make his paths straight.*" It is the voice of one "*crying in the wilderness,*" for he, like all of mankind, has his own doubts and demons, the creatures that inhabit our consciousness along with faith and hope. "*Repent!*" The voice cries. "*The kingdom of heaven is at hand.*" (Matt. 3.2) Turn about! Turn away from the lures of the world — power, money, prestige — they do not last.

This consciousness recognizes the need for cleansing the heart and mind, "*I baptize you with water for repentance,*" (Matt. 3.11) to confirm that one is ready and willing to turn hisr life about. This is a necessary step in preparation for a baptism yet to come.

It is to prepare the way, for the one who is mightier than John, who will *"baptize you with the Holy Spirit,* (the Wholeness of Spirit), *and fire."* (Luke 3.16)

Fire is a powerful cleansing and purifying element, and is a universal symbol of Spirit. It is a transforming agent that burns away the dross and reveals the pure gold of spiritual wholeness. It is this activity of spirit that is forever declaring, Behold! I make all things new.

The ritual of baptism confers upon the one being baptized a new identity, a new nature. Baptism with the Holy Spirit is recognition of one's essential being as a son, or daughter, of the Most High, one with the Wholeness of Spirit, the Holy Spirit.

The Unbroken Colt

Jesus was jolted from his reverie, and nearly unseated, when the unbroken colt he rode shied suddenly, startled by a cloak tossed in its path by an enthusiastic follower at the side of the road. The poor beast had never been ridden before and was skittish and confused by what was happening in its young life. Jesus stroked the animal's neck, and his touch quieted the beast.

He would have preferred to walk, but his disciples had felt that on this occasion it was more fitting that he should ride into Jerusalem.

To quiet them, as he had just quieted the colt, when they passed near Bethphage and Bethany, he sent two of them into the village ahead. He told them that they would find tied there a colt that had never been ridden. They were to untie it and bring it to him, and should anyone ask why they were doing it, they were to say, *"The Lord has need of it."* They did as he requested and returned with the colt. They had placed their cloaks on the animal's back, and Jesus had gotten astride the beast, and they continued on their way.

A CLOSER LOOK

One might well ask why this strange little aside is included in the story. It has the same fanciful kind of content as does a myth, that when viewed from a literal perspective leaves one's rational mind twisting in the wind. It seems that its meaning and purpose can only be arrived at by allowing the mind to play with the episode and its images as metaphor — its symbolic language.

The life of Jesus, as portrayed in the New Testament, is a living metaphor of the consciousness of the man, and everything that appears in the story is there for the purpose of revealing that evolving consciousness. All that is recorded of what he said and did was intended to teach the principles that lead to a life of mastery. Here we have some clues regarding the nature of the man and the state of mind displayed — the consciousness in play.

He began the journey walking, and very likely contemplating what lay ahead for him. They pass by Bethphage (*place of unripe fruit*), and Bethany (*house of distress*), near the Mt. of Olives (*illumined high place*). Jesus' ministry has spanned a brief three years, not long enough for that which he has taught to bear fruit. It is on the tree but not yet ripe (*Bethphage*), and he is distressed by that fact, and depressed (*Bethany*). But it is near the Mount of Olives (*high place*), and he also feels a sense of exaltation, a feeling that his destiny is wrapped up in this journey, that for this he was born.

His disciples, who perhaps sense this in their leader, suggest that he ride into the city. It is likely that they envision him arriving astride some magnificent animal appropriate for a king. But he has a different idea, and sends them on a mission to bring him the colt of an ass, an animal that has never been ridden.

Now the ass was a beast of burden common to the area. It was ridden by the elders and even royalty, but they would not have chosen to ride one that had not been broken. Their pride, their position in the world, their ego, would not have allowed them to do so.

Jesus chose this animal—obstinate, head-strong and unbroken—precisely because it was a perfect symbol for the animal aspect of human consciousness, and the unripe ego. Christ riding this beast is symbolic of the illumined mind's natural relationship to the ego, which must be subservient and responsive to the Higher Self if one is to travel to Jerusalem, (*place of peace*).

Jesus was the master of the understatement when it came to matters important to the ego, a lesson reflected over and over in his message. *"Beware of practicing your piety before men in order to be seen,"* and *"When you give alms, sound no trumpet."* (Matt. 6.1) His choice of a lowly beast of burden, an animal that had never been ridden before, is also symbolic of one being moved by that which is new in consciousness and purpose.

And when he suggested that should they be questioned as to why they were taking the colt, they were to say, "The Lord needs it," he was not speaking of himself. In metaphysical contemplation of the scriptures the word Lord is often looked at as being synonymous with the Law, the infallible action of God in the world — in all of creation. And Jesus came to fulfill the Law; therefore, *"The Lord has need of it."*

CHAPTER 8

The Wilderness Experience

Following his baptism by John, Jesus was
led by the Spirit into the wilderness, where he
fasted for forty days. The words he had heard,
*"This is my beloved son, in whom I am well
pleased,"* (Luke 3.22) had filled him with an
exquisite sense of intimacy with God. "My Father," he whispered, "My Father!" The sense of it
left him breathless. In the depths of him it resonated as truth, he knew it to be true, but his
mind struggled to wrap itself around that truth.
It had filled him with an overwhelming need to
be alone, away from the distractions of the
world, to be with this awesome power, and to
consider what he was to do with it.

Forty days he spent under the blazing
desert sun, with little shade for comfort, and
forty nights huddled in his heaviest cloak
against the desert chill. He fasted, wrapped in

prayer and meditation. He sat in the mouth of a small cave-like hollow, on the eastern slope of a rocky abutment, which afforded some shelter from the buffeting winds that rose from the desert floor below. The hours blurred into a monotonous flow of days and nights.

So deep was his meditation, his communion with God, that time itself seemed to vanish, and with it all the boundaries by which it is measured. He was vaguely aware of its passage only by the rays of the rising sun striking his face each dawn. Except for an occasional sip of water from a goatskin bag that lay beside him, he rarely moved. Even hunger, which had been a constant companion early on, receded and slipped into a familiar space, like the complaints of a noxious neighbor who one has learned to ignore.

The Temptations

But as the period of fasting and meditation came to a close, the hunger returned, more demanding. What he would not be willing to give for simple crust of bread. Might he not test it, this power, and this relationship? After all, whether he succeeded or failed, who would know? At the thought, a taunting voice had echoed in his head, *"If you are the Son of God, command these stones into loaves of bread."* (Matt.4.3)

But from deep within he heard yet another Voice, one that he would come to know and trust with his very life, and he responded, "*It is written that Man does not live by bread alone, but by every word that comes from the mouth of God.*'"

Now the tormenting voice seemed to take on a life of its own as it suggested yet another trial. "Well," it said, "turning stones into bread may not be enough of a test for one so favored." And Jesus was led to the edge of a deep canyon, where he was challenged, "*If you are the Son of God, throw yourself down, for it is written that He will give his angels charge of you, to guard you in all your ways. On their hands they will bear you up, lest you dash your foot against a stone.*" (Matt. 4.6) "You will not even so much as stub your toe," taunted the voice.

And again he heard the Voice from within, "It is written that you do not put the Lord your God to the test."

Not to be outdone, the tormentor said, "Well let me show you that for which powerful men throughout all time have struggled and fought, even killed, to obtain. *If you are the Son of God, worship me and all the power and splendor of all the kingdoms of the world can be yours.* (Matt. 4.8)

And yet again came the Voice from within, which had grown stronger with each challenge, and Jesus said, *"Away with you! It is written; worship the Lord your God, and serve him only.'"* And the taunting voice departed and was heard no more.

THE WILDERNESS – A CLOSER LOOK

Jesus' baptism left him overwhelmed by a wave of bliss that left him changed forever. The vision of the Holy Spirit, and the Voice from Heaven saying, "This is my beloved Son, with whom I am well pleased," had been so unexpected, it had left him stunned, and bewildered. He was "led up by the Spirit into the wilderness," and there he was "tempted by the Devil."

The wilderness is a place with which we are all familiar. Whenever life has touched us with an exalted vision, one that lifts us out of our ordinariness and seems too great to be true, we are likely to find ourselves in the wilderness. It is there that our doubts and questions assail us, and we are tempted. It is a devilish place to be.

Following forty long days and nights of fasting, Jesus was famished. He was hungry and was tempted to use the power vested in him by turning stones into loaves of bread. This temptation, as well as the others in the story, is blamed on the Devil, a creature thought to possess a power separate from God's. But, though there appears to be such in the affairs of man, it is an illusion.

There is only One God, by whatever name he may be called, all knowing, everywhere present and all-powerful. Man, who is made in the image and likeness of God, is an agent of that Power — a "beloved Son" (or Daughter). Unfortunately s/he, with rare exceptions, is ignorant of the nature of that Power, and of her relationship to it. All the evil in the world that s/he wishes to blame on the Devil is the result of that ignorance.

The possession of any power, whether temporal or spiritual, is sufficient in itself to give rise to the temptation for its abuse. And for one who possesses spiritual power, as does every man/woman if s/he but knew it, the voice of the tempter is never far away.

Man who is descended from Adam, eater of the tree of the knowledge of good and evil, needs no outside force to tempt him. His hunger for the things that power can bring is often insatiable, and that is temptation enough. He has no need for a devil.

Satan appears real enough in the life and affairs of man, for he is the personification of that ignorance and avarice that scars the life of unenlightened humankind. And the temptations are always the same regardless of the form they take. They are the thoughts and actions that ignore, violate, or misuse the Law apparent in the underlying principles of life—the Will of God.

When enlightened Jesus, the Christ, said, "*I am the life, the truth, and the way,*" he was declaring the truth about every living soul, if we but knew it and could accept it. We may be ignorant of it, even deny it, but the Holy Spirit hovers over the head of each of us, and the Voice from Heaven speaks to each of us when it declares, "This is my beloved Son (Daughter) in whom I am well pleased."

This may overwhelm us, as it did Jesus, and lead us into the wilderness where we are tempted to misuse it. But that truth and that voice will sustain us and we will emerge, as Jesus did, knowing the Christ within.

CHAPTER 9

The Twelve Are Chosen

With his disciples gathered about him they continued on their journey. He looked at each of them as they walked beside him, and the sounds of the crowd faded as he remembered where, and how, and why he had chosen these twelve.

When Jesus heard that John had been arrested, and imprisoned, he withdrew to Galilee, leaving Nazareth to make his home in Capernaum (*village of consolation*), by the sea. It was here, by the Sea of Galilee, that he took up the familiar cry of John, and began to proclaim, *"Repent, for the kingdom of heaven is at hand."* (Matt. 4.17) His ministry had begun.

Here beside the Sea of Galilee he began to teach. On one occasion the crowd was pressing close upon him to hear his words. He looked about for some space and saw two boats pulled up on the shore, where the fishermen were washing their nets. He got into one of the boats, the one belonging to Simon, and asked him to put out a little way from the shore. Then he sat down and taught the crowds from the boat.

When he had finished speaking, he said to Simon, "*Put out into the deep and let down your nets for a catch.*" (Luke 5.4) Simon was tired, and reluctant, for they had worked through the night and caught nothing. But there was something about this young rabbi that made it hard to refuse him, and Simon agreed and let down the nets. When they had done so, they caught so many fish that their nets were beginning to break. They frantically signaled their partners in the other boat to come and help, and with their help they filled both boats, to the point of sinking.

Simon and his brother Andrew were amazed at the catch of fish that they had taken, as were their partners James and John, sons of Zebedee. Their astonishment was mixed with fear. What manner of man was this? Simon fell to his knees before Jesus, saying, "*Go away from me Lord, for I am a sinful man.*" Jesus replied, "*Do not be afraid. Follow me and I will make you fishers of men.*" (Matt. 4.19)

They were astonished at this request, this invitation that sounded so like a command. They were fishermen and had worked all their young lives in order to make a decent living.

They owned their boats; they had responsibili-
ties to their families, to those they loved and
cared for. It was crazy. And if they did follow
him, where would he lead them, where was he
going? It was truly crazy.

But this was no ordinary man who stood
before them, waiting for their response. An aura
of power surrounded him; a magnetic force
seemed to radiate from him, that attracted them
like iron filings to a magnet. Each word he
spoke seemed filled with a strange, unearthly
power, as though spoken by God himself. What
was even more insane was that deep within each
of them sensed that this moment, this encounter and invitation, had been written in their
souls; that somehow the joining of their lives
with the life of this unusual man was foreordained, and that, a force was moving them that
they did not understand, but could not deny.
*"And when they had brought their boats to shore,
they left everything and followed him."* He had
chosen his first four disciples.

Attracted by the clarity and power and
freshness of what he taught, that which he
called "new wine," and amazed by the healing of
the sick that took place in his presence, the
numbers of those who followed grew daily. And
from these he chose eight more close disciples;
Matthew, Phillip, Bartholomew, Thomas, James
the son of Alphaeus, Simon who was called the

Zealot, Judas the son of James, and Judas Iscariot, who was to play an especially significant role in the unfolding drama of his life.

Twelve in all he selected, but he had not chosen any of them by chance. Each one represented a particular quality, a unique power, in man. These powers, these qualities, when woven together represented the elements of the discipline itself, of a life that leads to mastery.

They became like brothers and, under his daily guidance and instruction, had grown in ways they might never have conceived, as each added their unique talents to the whole. Together they had traveled throughout Galilee while Jesus taught in parables, proclaimed the power and authority of the Son of man, healed the sick and the lame, and preached the good news of the kingdom. His fame and notoriety as a charismatic leader who was adored by an ever-increasing number of followers, coupled with his unorthodox view of the relationship between God and man, had soon brought him to the attention of the religious authorities. He had not sought confrontation, nor had he avoided it. He went about teaching with an authority that was new and, for many, bordered on heresy.

THE DISCIPLES —
(QUALITIES OF MIND AND HEART)

Each of the disciples represented a quality of mind and heart, of Spirit, as reflected in the meaning of his name. Simon (hearkening, obeying), the first disciple chosen, Jesus later renamed Peter, which means rock. He is symbolic of that quality of listening and acceptance of the Word, wherein the Word becomes firm, like a rock. When the Word, the teaching, is received and obeyed in this way faith like a rock (Peter), is the result. Andrew, Simon's brother, is strength, while James and John, sons of Zebedee, mean judgment, discrimination, and love. The spiritual quality, that these first four disciples represent, provides a solid foundation for any discipline, but most certainly for one of a spiritual nature. Every discipline has at its core such an invisible foundation.

This foundation is doubly important, for it colors and gives a particular impetus to the rest of the powers (disciples). The eight additional disciples represent qualities of mind and heart needed to complete the foundation created by the first four. This is vital, for faith (Peter) that is not given direction by wisdom and love, can be turned into an awesome force of destruction.

The qualities that these eight brought, based on the meaning of their names, are as follows. Phillip, lover of horses, refers to the physi-

cal power in man, often symbolized by the horse in dream and mythology. Matthew, *gift of God,* refers to the faculty of *will.* Thomas means *conjoined* or *twin,* and refers to *understanding,* which in the best of circumstances is conjoined with *will* (Matthew). Bartholomew is *son of furrows, a field ready for seed,* refers to *imagination,* while James, the son of Alphaeus, is *order.* It is not surprising that Simon, the Zealot, implies *zeal.* Judas, the son of James, is the *power of renunciation,* and Judas Iscariot, the last disciple to be called means *man of conveniences,* and refers to the faculty of *acquisitiveness.* Taken together they represent the qualities of mind and heart, of spirit, that must be brought to *any* discipline where mastery is the objective.

It was significant, in the course of events, that John the Baptist was arrested and imprisoned *before* Jesus began his ministry. Jesus picked up where John left off, with the very same proclamation, "Repent! The kingdom of heaven is at hand." The story required this sequence of events, and the same is true in the inner life of man. The awakened intellect (John the Baptist) must be restrained before the spiritual man, (the Christ), can assume the mantle of leadership. John foresaw this when he baptized Jesus; *"He must increase, but I must decrease."* (John 3.30)

CHAPTER 10

Jerusalem

A great shout went up from the crowd that shook him from his reverie. He was astonished at the number of people who lined the road singing and crying out, "*Blessed is the king who comes in the name of the Lord! Peace in heaven and glory in the highest.*" (Luke 19.38) Some of the Pharisees in the crowd were upset by this and asked Jesus to tell his followers to stop. He replied, "*I tell you, if these were silent, the very stones would cry out.*" (Luke 19.40)

Jerusalem, the holy city, now lay before them burnished golden in the morning sun. As he looked upon the city, a great sadness swept over him and he wept and cried out, "*Would that even today you knew the things that make for peace! But now they are hid from your eyes.*" (Luke 19.42) The temple, with its dazzling dome reaching into the sky, seemed to beckon the surging throng that poured through the city's gates. He pressed on as he felt a great need to enter into his Father's house.

When they reached the entrance to the city, they were carried on the crest of a surging wave of people through the gate and into the midst of a yet more closely packed crowd. It was the feast of Passover, and the city was bulging with people from all over the region. There was a high emotional pitch to the crowd. And when they saw the man, their comments could be heard. "There he is. That's him, Jesus of Nazareth! They say he performs miracles; heals the sick, raises the dead." "You fool! What good has ever come out of Nazareth?" Hands reached for him, and behind the hands, pleading eyes, "Heal me, Lord!" *"Blessed is he who comes in the name of the Lord."* (Matt. 21.9)

His disciples brushed their comments, and their pleas, aside as they formed a protective circle about him. With the towering Simon Peter in the lead, joined by his brother Andrew, they cut their way through the throng to the steps of the temple, and entered into the outer courtyard.

The Cleansing of the Temple

The crowd inside was hardly less than that which they had just left. The tables of the moneychangers were crowded and busy, for no one could offer a sacrifice that wasn't purchased with the special coinage of the temple. And the exchange was always weighted to the benefit of the temple's coffers — cheating was rampant.

Jesus and his disciples stood just inside the entrance. As he looked upon the scene before him, a quiet fury swelled within him that brought a flush to his cheeks and a fearsome light to his eyes. With a loud cry, filled with anger mixed with anguish, he said, "It is written; My house shall be a house of prayer, but you have made it a den of robbers." (Luke 19.46)

And with that he walked quickly to the nearest table and, with a mighty heave, turned it upside down. And like the sweep of a mighty wind, he went from table to table, until all were turned upside down, while those that had tended them cowered before his wrath. It was an action of open confrontation and challenge that would lead eventually to his death, but for the time being it went unchallenged.

Thereafter he taught daily in the temple, and *"The blind and the lame came to him in the temple, and he healed them."* (Matt. 21.14) But when the chief priests and the scribes saw the amazing things that he did, and heard the children cry out in the temple, *"Hosanna to the Son of David,"* they became angry and said to him, *"Do you hear what these are saying?"* Jesus said to them, *"Yes; have you never read, 'Out of the mouths of babes thou hast brought perfect praise?'"* Matt. 21.15) He left them and went out of the city to Bethany, where he spent the night.

THE TEMPLE

When Jesus grieved at the sight of Jerusalem, *place of peace*, it was with the sad realization that the prevalent conditions of the city were such that peace was not to be had without significant change. The city and country lived under the heel of Roman rule, but this was not of major concern to Jesus. His concern was with the heart and soul of the city, its spiritual well- being. Upon arriving in the city, his very first act addressed the problem head-on — the cleansing of the Temple.

The Temple is a powerful symbol of that sacred space in mind, in consciousness, where one goes to enter *"the kingdom of God."* It is a place of worship, and of communion, that Jesus found had been turned into a den of thieves. It was now a place where money and greed reigned supreme. Those who entered with a spiritual hunger, instead of being fed, were routinely coerced and fleeced. Not only had the people been cheated, but the Temple itself was desecrated, its real purpose subverted.

This situation occurs in the realm of mind, in the inner life of man, when the spiritual impulse has been replaced, overwhelmed, by the desire to turn everything into a profit. All the available energy and space is given over to material gain. It is a condition in which one is robbed of the opportunity to honor and receive spiritual nourishment. The kingdom of heaven, that sacred space that is to be found within one's self, is not at hand. Only a complete turnabout, an *overthrowing* of the conditions, can heal the situation. When Jesus overturned the tables of the money-changers, it was an act symbolic of repentance, a turning about, an overturning of those conditions and activities that rob one of the experiences of the sacred. It is a cleansing of the temple of all but that for which it is intended. There is a proper venue in one's life for the marketplace, and its purpose, but it is *not* the Temple —the sacred space in one's life.

Whenever we take a practice, or ritual, that is intended to be sacred, and prostitute it, we are the same as those that Jesus found in the Temple. If we join a church for the purpose of developing contacts to further our career, our finances, we have turned the house of prayer into a den of thieves. And when a church, or temple, is more focused on the bottom line than it is on being a house of prayer and healing, it has become a den of thieves, and most certainly no place of peace.

"*And the blind and the lame came to him in the temple, and he healed them.*" We are not among those who would question that those who were physically lame and blind were healed by this incredible soul, but there is more to this simple line of scripture. Lameness and blindness are apt metaphors for a host of limitations we find when we consider the mental, emotional, and spiritual conditions commonly encountered in life.

We go to the physician for *curing* the physical ills of the body, but we go to the *Temple* for *healing* the inner life. Where do you go to be healed of your blindness or lameness in these areas of experience, if not to the temple? And would it not be wise for you not seek out such a one as Jesus, someone wise and loving, someone who has spent some serious time in the temple?

Jesus often said, "*Your faith has made you well.*" And it is faith that *always* makes you well, for it is inherent in every action you take in order to gain relief. The simple decision to take an aspirin for your headache is an act of faith. You would not take it if you did not have some measure of faith that it would bring relief. And faith is a quality that is only found in the temple, a sacred space within, no matter where you may be physically. First seek the kingdom of God, which is within — as is the Christ.

The Cursing of the Fig Tree

In the morning, as he was returning to Jerusalem, he was hungry and saw a fig tree. He went to the tree intent on satisfying his hunger with some sweet figs. When he found only leaves, he cursed the tree, saying, *"May no fruit ever come from you again!"* (Matt. 21.19) And before their very eyes, the fig tree withered.

His disciples were astonished at what they had just witnessed, and well they might be. This was a man who loved life, and spoke of love as the most essential element in life, who had just cursed a living thing. This man, who had given thanks and blessed a few fish and loaves that fed thousands, had cursed this tree *to its roots*, and it had immediately withered. Astonished at what they had just seen, his disciples asked Jesus, *"How did the fig tree wither at once?"*

He answered them, *"Truly I tell you, if you have faith and do not doubt, not only will you do what has been done to the fig tree, but even if you say to this mountain, 'Be lifted up and thrown into the sea,' it will be done. Whatever you ask for in prayer with faith, you will receive."* (Matt. 21.18 – 22)

THE LESSON OF THE FIG TREE

Here we have yet another episode in the narrative that does not seem to add anything of importance to the unfolding events. Jesus acted in a way that seems completely foreign to his nature when he cursed a living thing. It astonished and bewildered his disciples

On the surface, it was a very human response to the disappointment and frustration of failing to find that which would appease his hunger. It is refreshing and enlightening to catch a glimpse of the human side of this remarkable man.

Jesus was fully under siege, mentally and emotionally pressed to the limit by the threat he knew lay ahead. He was a man, after all, and subject to all of the emotions of men. He had certainly been angry with the moneychangers in the temple. His failure to find any figs on the tree might have been the proverbial "last straw," and in a brief moment of forgetfulness his reaction was to curse tree. But a closer look reveals another possibility.

He was ever the teacher, and when his disciples asked about his action and its result, he turned the situation into one that revealed a powerful truth. It was a lesson about faith, and about the power of the word when spoken in faith. He said to them that if they had faith, and did not doubt, they could do what he had done to the fig tree or, move a mountain. He told them, *"Whatever you ask for in prayer with faith, you will receive."* (Matt. 21.22)

The principle stated here is; that which we curse withers and that which we bless prospers. In the Old Testament we find, *"I set before you a blessing and a curse;"* with the instruction to choose. (Deut. 11.26) Life is forever doing this very thing. When we understand that we have a choice regarding our response, and that how we respond will largely determine how we will experience the matter, we assume a position of power as to the outcome.

We find the basis for this principle set forth in Genesis. First, the power that is vested in every living soul is that conferred by our identity, *"made in the image and likeness of God."* We are each a son or daughter of the living God, vested with the same creative power that in the beginning said, "Let there be ..." and there was. Such is the power of the Word spoken in full faith and acceptance of that which it declares. Out of our use of this power we create our world, by naming it.

And we see that power given to Adam when God brought all the creatures of the world to him to see what he would *name* them. And whatever he named them, *that was their name.* (Gen. 2.19)

We make that critical choice between a blessing and a curse the moment we name a situation or circumstance, for as with Adam, the name reflected the nature of the creature.

When life happens and we name it "bad," we live with, and experience, it as bad. When the same thing happens and we name it "good," we live with, and experience the good. What is placed before us is just the is-ness of life, the content. What is — **is**. By naming it we place it in a context of good or bad, for us or against us, and then we proceed to live out the experience within that context.

Like an artist we take our personal perception of what life places before us and we frame it, and name it. When we do this we declare our belief about it, and then we proceed to live out that belief.

This aligns with the universal law, "*As you believe, so is it done unto you*" (Mark 11.23). We are forever living out our beliefs. And when we realize that this activity of naming is a constant in our life, we may realize that we might well be cursing the very place where we look for our good — cursing it "to its roots."

The Challenge

Everyday thereafter Jesus could be found teaching in the temple, surrounded by crowds that grew daily. The people were spellbound.

This infuriated the chief priests and scribes who, while they looked for ways to kill him, feared moving openly against him. Accompanied by the elders, they sought to undermine his credibility. They asked him, "*Tell us, by what authority are you doing these things? Who is it who gave you this authority?*" (Luke 20.1)

He responded by asking them a question, a tactic he often used in answering those who sought to lay a trap for him. He asked, "*Did the baptism of John come from heaven, or was it of human origin?*" The question presented them with a dilemma. If they said from heaven, he would ask them why they did not believe John. If they said of human origin, they feared the people would stone them, for the people believed that John was a prophet. So they answered that they did not know where it came from. Then Jesus quietly said to them, "*Neither will I tell you by what authority I am doing these things.*" (Luke 20.8)

BY WHAT AUTHORITY

This question concerning one's authority is a common reaction that occurs whenever the old is challenged by the new, whether in the outer world, or the inner life of man. All organized effort religious, political, or personal establishes and defends a power base, an authority.

Each begins with an idea, a concept, around which there gathers a structure of supporting ideas, all of which results in a creed, a doctrine, a mission statement, a purpose. Each creates its own truth, rightness and authority, which it will then defend against all threats and challenges. This dynamic occurs in the individual, as well as in consortiums of all kinds.

In the individual it is the ego, the sense of self, that issues the challenge, and as with any organization its primary objective is survival. Nowhere is this more pronounced than in religious organizations, where faith in their particular doctrine is vital to their survival. This is equally true in the inner life of man.

The discipline that Jesus offered as the Way to live is filled with elements that shake the Ego, the individual established power base, to its core. Anything that threatens custom, tradition, habit, the established way, is suspect. In the inner life of man it is the Ego, representative of the status quo, that challenges the Christ, the Higher Self, with the question about authority. One can understand the fear that the ego feels at the threat of being replaced, just as one can appreciate the fear that drove the chief priests and elders to decide that the only solution was to kill Jesus. The ego is intent on the same concerning the Christ.

The Plot

There were two days left before the Passover and the chief priests and elders of the people, infuriated by the actions of this upstart rabbi, gathered in the palace of the high priest, Caiaphas, where they conspired to arrest Jesus and kill him. They agreed that it could not be done during the festival, for this could cause a riot among the people. It would have to be done carefully, preferably under cover of darkness. They had their spies placed among the followers of Jesus looking for any who were discontent, or disillusioned. They found what they were looking for in the person of Judas Iscariot, one of the twelve.

A recent episode had served to confirm his discontent and to lay the foundation for the betrayal of the man Jesus, for a price. It had happened in Bethany while Jesus was visiting the house of Simon the leper. A woman had come up to him carrying an alabaster flask of very expensive ointment, which she applied to Jesus' head, as he sat at table.

His disciples were stunned and indignant at the apparent waste, for the ointment could have been sold for a large sum of money, and given to the poor. None was more indignant than Judas Iscariot, who was the keeper of the purse and manager of the resources of the twelve.

131

Jesus had responded to their concern, saying, "*Why do you trouble the woman, for she has done a beautiful thing to me. For you will always have the poor with you, but you will not always have me.*" (Matt. 26.11) His answer did not entirely satisfy them. It only added to the disappointment in the mind of some of them who had begun to see that his mission was not that of a conquering hero who would free them from the yoke of Rome and restore Israel to its former greatness.

Those thoughts and ambitions became evident when the mother of John and James approached Jesus with a request. When he asked her what she wanted, she said, "*Declare that these two sons of mine will sit, one at your right hand and one at your left, in your kingdom.*" With a sad gentleness in his voice, Jesus said to her, "*You do not know what you are asking.*" Jesus knew that she, like the vast majority of his followers, was unaware of what lay before him, or what his true mission was to be.

Then to the two brothers he said, "*Are you able to drink the cup that I am about to drink?*" (Matt. 20.22) When they said they were able, an even deeper sadness filled his words when he told them that they would indeed drink the same cup, but that where they were to sit was not his to grant.

When the other disciples heard this they were very angry with James and John. For the truth was that these same thoughts and ambitions had played about in the mind of each of them at one time or another. For they, like most of his followers, saw in Jesus, the Messiah, the Anointed One, the powerful king that they had so long awaited. The stage was set.

The Bargain is Struck

At the first opportunity, Judas Iscariot met with the chief priests and officers of the temple police and offered to lead them to Jesus for a price. He was paid thirty pieces of silver, and warned that should he fail to fulfill his part of the bargain he would not live long enough to spend any of it. From that moment on he began to look for an opportunity to betray Jesus.

Do this in remembrance of me.

CHAPTER 11

The Passover

Then came the day of Unleavened Bread, on which the Passover lamb had to be sacrificed, and Jesus said to Peter and John, *"Go and prepare the Passover meal for us that we may eat it."* They asked him where it was to be held, and. Jesus, who knew that they were being watched, told them that a man carrying a jar of water would meet them, and they were to follow him into the house he entered. They were to ask the owner Jesus and his disciples were to eat the Passover. They did as Jesus instructed, and were shown a furnished upper room, where they made the preparations for the Passover meal.

That evening, in order to avoid attracting undue attention, they made their way singly and in pairs to the meeting place, and to the upper room and the Passover meal. They sat together at a table laden with roasted lamb, unleavened bread, and wine. Jesus sat in their midst, with John sitting close at his side. If he had a favorite it was John, the youngest of the twelve, who was devoted to him with the pure heart and passion that only the young seem to possess.

Jesus said, *"I have eagerly desired to eat this Passover with you, for we shall not meet like this again until all is fulfilled."* His next words left them speechless, for he told that that there was one among them who would him, who had already betrayed him in his heart. (Luke 22.14)

A chorus of denials and dismay erupted from his disciples at this astonishing announcement. One after the other they cried out, *"Surely not I, Lord?"* Jesus answered, *"The one who has dipped his hand into the bowl with me will betray me."* He knew that this too was foreordained, for he then said, *"The Son of Man goes as it is written of him, but woe to that one by whom he is betrayed! It would have been better for that one not to have been born."* (Luke 22.21) The disciples looked at each other, questioning who it might be, each one affirming his faithfulness and loyalty more insistently.

With a mixture of love and sadness, Jesus looked into the eyes of each of the twelve, for he knew who was to betray him. Word had reached him from inside the inner circles of the priests and elders, for not everyone there wished him ill, or agreed with the plan to kill him.

Judas Iscariot said, *"Surely not I, Rabbi?"* And Jesus answered, *"You have said so."* His traitorous act exposed to all present, Judas fled in shame. And then the disciples began to argue as to which one of them would be regarded as the greatest, but they became quiet and thoughtful when Jesus said; *"The greatest among you must become like the youngest, and the leader like one who serves."* (Luke 22.25)

Do This in Remembrance

While they were eating, Jesus took a loaf of bread, and then after blessing it he broke it, gave it to the disciples, and said, *"Take, eat; this is my body."* Then he took a cup and, after giving thanks, gave it to them, saying, *"Drink from it, all of you; for this is my blood of the covenant. Do this in remembrance of me."* (Luke 22.19)

The sacredness, the intimacy of this ritual, struck deep within their hearts. Sobered by it, and by the revelations of the evening, they quietly sang a hymn and then together, went out with Jesus to the Mount of Olives.

THE PASSOVER – A CLOSER LOOK

The Passover, which literally means a passing over, or an overcoming, was an annual celebration of Jews that commemorated their escape from slavery in Egypt. It fits neatly into the story of Jesus, for he knew that with his betrayal he was on the threshold of such a movement — the ultimate passing over.

In the larger sense this "passing over" is a perfect metaphor for any shift in consciousness along life's path. In the course of any life there is a passing over from one stage to another; from infancy to the age of reason, from childhood to adolescence, and so on. Each change carries with it a greater sense of freedom and autonomy. And then there are those episodes when one passes from the bondage of an addiction to freedom, an overcoming. This was an underlying theme in the life of the Master, reflected in what he taught and in the manner in which he lived. *"I am come that you might have life, and have it more abundantly."* (John 10.10)

They met in an *upper room* of the house. All events of a sacred nature, like prayer, meditation, and communion with God always take place in an elevated space. Whenever one aspires in mind and heart to an upward reach toward the highest and best, toward communion with their God, they move to an upper room. Throughout scripture, particularly the parables of Jesus, it is common to find *household* used as a metaphor for one's mind-set, one's state of consciousness.

Fully aware of what awaited him Jesus initiated a ritual of communion with his disciples, which he asked them to do in remembrance of him.　He broke bread into pieces and gave a piece to each of his disciples, saying that it was his body.　And then he offered them a chalice filled with wine, and asked them to drink, saying, *"this is my blood of the covenant."* The power and beauty of this ritual, this sacred practice, becomes clear in its mystical implications when we look at *bread, wine,* and *blood* for their symbolic intent.

Bread is the most common symbol for substance; "Give us this day our daily bread." And body is more than the flesh of a person; it is the substance of the very life, nature, work, and all that s/he has stood for in their living. When one remembers and communes with *that* body, s/he honors and embraces the totality of the person.

And wine is that perfect symbol of Spirit. When Jesus turned the water into wine at the wedding in Cana, he transformed the life-giving qualities of water (consciousness) into the spiritual, and it became a sweet wine. It is *this* wine that Jesus offered for each of them to drink as, the blood of the covenant.

Blood is the most powerful symbol of life itself, and here Jesus offered his life, "my blood," as dedicated to the covenant. And what was the covenant, his mission?　It was, *"I am come that they might have life, and have it more abundantly."* (John 10.10)　When one remembers and communes with *that* wine, they honor and embrace the totality of *that* Spirit.

The Desertion of the Disciples

Jesus was aware that the revelations of this night had shaken them all to the core. He said, "*You will all become deserters because of me this night; for it is written, I will strike the shepherd, and the sheep of the flock will be scattered.*" (Matt. 26.30) They each again declared their loyalty and steadfast love, and none more loudly than Peter, who said, "*Though all become deserters because of you, I will never desert you.*"

Jesus, knowing the kind of terror that this night would produce, told Peter that "*this very night, before the cock crows, you will deny me three times.*" Peter replied, "*Even though I must die with you, I will not deny you.*" (Matt. 26.35) These words were echoed by all the disciples.

THE DESERTION – A CLOSER LOOK

When Jesus gathered with his disciples for the Passover meal, he sat in their midst. He surrounded himself with *faith* (Peter), *strength* (Andrew), *judgment* (James), *love* (John), *understanding* (Thomas), *motivation* (Phillip), *will* (Matthew), *imagination* (Bartholomew), *order* (James the son of Alphaeus), *enthusiasm* (Simon the Zealot), *renunciation* (Judas the son of James), and *acquisitiveness* (Judas Iscariot). He sat in the midst of every quality of mind and heart necessary for one to achieve mastery within the discipline that he taught and lived.

John (*Love*), his favorite, sat closest to him at the Passover meal. It is this quality that is the foundation, the very heart, of his life and teaching. It is the essence of the one commandment that he taught and embraced. *"Love God with all your heart, your mind, and your might, and love your neighbor as yourself."* (Luke 10.27)

The disciples had argued with each other as to who was the greatest, and the same argument often plays out in the inner life of man where these qualities appear to have a life of their own. These living entities, these "other selves," often seem to argue among themselves as to who is the most important in one's life. And, depending on what is going on in one's life at any given moment we are likely to see one as being, for that moment at least, more important than the others.

For example, I might *desire* (Judas Iscariot) to write a book and have some measure of *faith* (Peter) that I am capable of doing so. If the desire is weak and the faith is tepid, I might never actually begin the act of writing. I need to *understand* (Thomas) that a half-hearted *desire* (Judas Iscariot) to write will not be sufficient.

I may be *motivated* (Phillip), even become *enthusiastic* (Simon, the Zealot), as I *imagine*

(Bartholomew) the rewards of being a successful author and yet fail to bring the necessary *order* (James, the son of Alphaeus), to my life to make room for a regular writing schedule.

My *judgment* (James) is that I need to *renounce* (Judas, the son of James) time-consuming activities, like hours of mindless television, and dedicate them to writing. Finally I am going to need the *will* (Matthew) to summon the *strength* (Andrew), and the self-*love* (John) to be both persistent and patient in the process of writing every day, to bring me back again and again to the keyboard.

It is clear that they are all needed, and that each serves best by bringing their own unique quality to the whole. Christ taught that the greatest among them must become like the youngest, and the leader like one who serves. Each of the powers, with the possible exception of love, is capable of betraying one, of deserting the spiritual for the material temporal world. But, of all of them, the desire to possess, *acquisitiveness*, can prove to be the most troublesome and greatest hindrance to the successful completion of a project, or to growth in spiritual awareness.

But Judas Iscariot was only the first of his disciples to desert Jesus. When the full weight and anger of the establishment appeared about to crush them, along with Jesus, they all deserted him. This is a common experience in the life of most individuals. When we find ourselves in the midst of that life experience that we know as the *dark night of the soul,* it is then that all our vaunted powers (disciples) seem to disappear. That is the dark night when they all *fall away.*

All who have experienced that moment when everything they have worked for, hoped for, and dreamed of lies shattered and in pieces around their feet, know of this desertion. In that instant one's very identity, the structure around which one has formed a life is challenged to the point of annihilation. .

It is a night, not unlike that night in Gethsemane, when we are faced with a situation that is so heavy in its demands, so stressful, that we feel devoid of any hope. Our vaunted strengths and abilities seem as nothing. We are left bereft of all our resources; our *faith* is shaken, our *will* is weak, our *judgment* questionable, *order* has been replaced with chaos, and our *imagination* is engaged in playing out the worst of scenarios. We are left with nothing to do but pray. Only love (John) is left standing at the foot of the cross, and ultimately only love can save us.

My Father, if it be possible, let this cup pass from me; nevertheless not as I will, but as thou wilt.

I will, to will, thy will.

CHAPTER 12

Jesus in Gethsemane

Then Jesus went with them to a garden called Gethsemane, taking with him Peter, and James and John, the sons of Zebedee. He said to them, "*Sit here while I go over there and pray.*" (Matt. 26.36) Deeply distraught at the thought of what lay in store for him, he asked them to remain nearby, and to stay awake with him. Going a little farther, he threw himself on the ground and prayed, "*My Father, if it is possible, let this cup pass from me; yet not what I want but what you want.*" (Matt. 26.39) When he returned to the disciples and found them sleeping, he said to Peter, "*So, could you not stay awake with me one hour?*"

Once again he asked that they stay awake, and told them to pray that they not be caught up in the trials that he faced, and added, "*the spirit indeed is willing, but the flesh is weak.*" For

a second time he went and prayed, *"My Father, if this cannot pass unless I drink it, your will be done."* Upon his return he again found them sleeping. Without waking them, he went yet again and prayed for the third time, the same prayer. This time when he returned he said to his disciples, *"Are you still sleeping and taking your rest? Look now and see the hour is at hand, and the Son of Man is betrayed into the hands of sinners. Get up, my betrayer is at hand."*
(Matt. 26.45)

JESUS PRAYED, AND DISCIPLES SLEPT

Jesus knew that he would be betrayed, and he knew the likely outcome of that betrayal. The knowledge filled him with a profound grief, and a wish that it might somehow be avoided, or at least postponed. His ministry had been so short, there was so much more he had hoped to do, to share. Does it have to be this way, he wondered? All the while he was filled with the sense that this was his destiny that was written in the book of life at the beginning of beginnings.

He had asked Peter (*faith*), James (*judgment, wisdom*), and John (*love*), to "watch with him" for a time while he prayed. These three disciples represented three powers, qualities of mind and heart that anyone who faced a crisis would want to be present, and awake. Three times he went to pray and, each time upon his return, he found them sleeping. The qualities of faith, judgment, and love, which could be a comfort to him, powers that are sorely needed to "watch with him" while he prayed, have in their own fashion deserted him. And the moment of his betrayal is at hand.

Betrayed With a Kiss

The chief priests and elders had Judas picked up and brought before them, where he was told that it was time for him to earn the money he had been paid. He was now to lead them to the man, Jesus.

Judas, now overcome with shame and guilt from his exposure as a traitor at the Passover meal, had second thoughts. He took the thirty pieces of silver, money that now burned in his hand like the fires of Hell, and threw them at the feet of Caiaphas. "I don't want your money," he cried. "I can't do this. Find another!" He screamed, as he fell to his knees before them.

Caiaphas was unmoved by his pleas, and with contempt dripping from every word, he said, "Oh, you will keep the bargain you have made, or you will not live to see the dawn." Then to his Captain of the guard he said, "Take this miserable creature and see that he does as he has agreed."

The soldiers grabbed Judas and yanked him to his feet. The leader put a dagger to his throat and growled, "Where is the man Jesus to be found?" Judas whimpered, "Gethsemane." With him firmly in their grasp they left.

The soldiers were armed with swords, while the others who joined them along the way carried clubs or torches. There was no moon, and the night closed in about them as they came to the outskirts of the garden. In the limited light of the torches, the garden appeared empty. Had the wretch lied, the Captain wondered, as again he drew the dagger from his belt.

Just then someone at the edge of their group cried out, "There! There they are, over there!" and pointed to several indistinct figures in the darkness. As they moved closer, Judas pointed and said, "That's him. That's Jesus in the middle," and tried to free himself from the grasp of the Captain. "Not so fast, worm," the officer hissed into his ear. "If I take in the wrong man, it will be on my head." He added, "I want no mistake, you will kiss the man we seek." With that he thrust Judas forward toward Jesus and his disciples.

With tears streaming down his face Judas went and stood before Jesus, who said, *"Friend, do what you are here to do."* Judas, his voice choked with emotion, said, *"Greetings, Rabbi,"* and kissed him. The officer stepped forward and arrested Jesus.

BETRAYAL – AN INSIDE JOB

In each life it is acquisitiveness *(Judas Iscariot)*, insatiable desire, that will betray one on the path to mastery, to spiritual awakening -- to the Christ. Judas Iscariot is a living metaphor for that condition of mind and heart that is most intent on acquiring worldly power and wealth. It was he who carried the purse for the disciples in their travels together, and it was he, perhaps more than any of the other disciple, who carried the image of Jesus as the one to reign over the house of David, truly king of the Jews.

The amount of money involved here was paltry in the light of the terrible deed he had agreed to do, but it is significant to *our* story. It points to a classic collision of values, the temporal as opposed to the spiritual. Even the phrase, "thirty pieces of silver," usually uttered with contempt, has become a metaphor for how cheaply one can be bought by the world's trinkets, to betray the best in us.

Who in their lifetime has not fallen prey to the lure of money offered for a particular job, or for an action, which they knew in their heart, or subsequently painfully learned, was a betrayal of their highest and best. In that instant one becomes Judas Iscariot to the Christ within.

The enticement for Judas was more complex than the amount of money, for behind the money was the established power structure that wore the face of religion, the face of *righteous-ness*. With the forces in play, Judas might well feel that it was Jesus who has betrayed him, and all the others who had followed, into thinking that he was bringing about an earthly kingdom where he would rule, and they beside him.

The fear and fury of the chief priests and elders is the typical reaction of any established power base in the world, or in the inner life of man. The ego-centered individual with his personal doctrine of *truth* and *rightness*, that has proven to be successful in the world of affairs, is deeply rooted in his established power base. Anything that threatens that doctrine is to be eliminated.

A fascinating aspect of our story, and one that clearly plays out in the inner life of man, is that the Promise (here the Christ vision and way of life), is betrayed from *within*. Christ is identified and *betrayed* by one of his disciples. It is one of the elements of the *discipline* itself that provides the opening, the chink in the armor.

When one embarks on a path to mastery of any discipline, and is *arrested* in his progress, it is always due to the desertion, the *betrayal*, of one of the essential elements of the discipline. The disciples represent those qualities of the mind and heart that are needed to fulfill the Promise. The *betrayal* is always an inner event, for it always involves the desertion of one of these needed qualities (disciples). And it always comes in the *dark of night*, when the lack of *light* (insight) makes it hard to *see* and *identify* the Promise, the vision of the higher good.

It is then that our vision of the Promise is most vulnerable. We *know* it is coming, as did Jesus, and we know the source of our betrayal even as we pray that it might pass. But we are also aware that the will of God, the immutable action of universal law, is at work. In that light we might see it as the fulfillment of prophecy, as did Jesus on that fateful night.

All the events taking place in the outer world are the result of the activity of forces, of invisible energy patterns, in play in the inner realms of consciousness of the individual, and of the collective. The individual is a microcosm of the macrocosm, an integral part of the Whole. *All* of it acts, and reacts, according to an invisible set of laws or principles, which one might see as the will of God in action. This story, this journey, this life, is a living metaphor of that greater truth. Each life is.

An Act of Resistance

Suddenly, at the sight of his beloved teacher being manhandled, one of those with Jesus drew a sword and struck the slave of the high priest, cutting off his ear. Jesus cried, "*No more of this! All who take the sword will perish by the sword."* Then he said, *"Do you think that I cannot appeal to my Father, and he will at once send me more than twelve legions of angels? But if I did that how would the scripture be fulfilled, which say it must happen in this way?"* He turned to the crowd and said, *"Have you come out with swords and clubs to arrest me as though I were a bandit? While I was with you daily in the temple, you did not lay hands on me, but this hour and the power of darkness are yours."* And they seized him and took him away.

THE TWO-EDGED SWORD

You live by the sword, you die by the sword, is a statement of universal Law. That violence begets violence is obvious to anyone who looks at the history of man, or at the current state of the world. There are some clear and powerful symbols in this brief account.

The sword sliced off the *ear* of the slave, and by some accounts it was the *right* ear. The primary result as well as the continuing dynamic of any outbreak of violence is the inability of the antagonists to *hear* one another

Jesus commanded that the violence stop and he healed the injury, restoring the man's ear — his *hearing*. Above all Jesus wanted his message to be *rightly* heard, especially by those in whom it had generated such fear and misunderstanding.

The sword, in myth and dream, is a symbol of that faculty of mind that is discerning, discriminating, incisive. These are excellent skills but are ill-suited to handle emotionally charged situations like the arrest of Jesus. What is required is a more holistic approach, a view that sees beyond the tensions and heightened emotions of the moment. Jesus' vision, clearly holistic, removes one from the eye of the storm, and reveals a broader, deeper, perspective. There is that ability in the truly wise, like the Master Teacher, to be at the center of a confrontation and yet achieve the psychic distance necessary to see the whole of a thing, and bring healing to it.

If you are the Christ, tell us.

*If I tell you, you will not believe; and
if I ask you, you will not answer.
But from now on the Son of man
shall be seated at the right hand of
the power of God.*

CHAPTER 13

The Trials Begin

Those who had arrested Jesus took him to Caiaphas, the high priest, in whose house the scribes and the elders had gathered. All the disciples had deserted Jesus, with exception of Peter who followed at a distance. When Peter reached the courtyard of the high priest, he went inside and sat among the guards to see what transpired.

The chief priests, and the whole council, were looking for false testimony against Jesus so that they might put him to death. Many came forward to testify thinking that they would curry favor with the chief priests and council, but they were not credible. Finally there were two who came forward and said, *"This fellow said, 'I am able to destroy the temple of God and to build it in three days."*

The high priest leaped to his feet and asked Jesus, "*Have you no answer? What is it that they testify against you?*" Jesus remained silent, while looking directly into the eyes of the high priest. Caiaphas was clearly unsettled by the silent Jesus who stood before unmoved and untouched by the hate and fear that filled the room around him. He shouted, "*I put you under oath before the living God, tell us if you are the Messiah, the Son of God.*" Jesus replied, "*If I tell you, you will not believe; and if I question you, you will not answer. But from now on the Son of Man will be seated at the right hand of the power of God.*" (Luke 22.69)

Others shouted, "*Are you, then, the Son of God?*" He replied, "*You say that I am.*" Then the high priest tore his clothes and screamed, "*He has blasphemed! Why do we still need witnesses? You have now heard his blasphemy. What is your verdict?*" They shouted, "*Death! He deserves death.*" With that they surged around Jesus and struck him, spat upon him, and mocked him, "*You, Messiah, prophesy to us! Who is it that struck you?*"

Peter's Denial of Jesus

Now Peter, who still sat outside in the courtyard, could hear what was taking place within. A servant-girl approached him and said, *"You also were with Jesus the Galilean."* Peter replied, *"I do not know what you are talking about."* He went out to the porch where another servant saw him, and said, to the bystanders, *"This man was with Jesus of Nazareth."* Peter swore an oath; *"I do not know the man."* After a little while others who gathered there came up and said to Peter, *"Certainly you are also one of them, for your accent betrays you."* Peter began to curse, and he swore yet again, *"I do not know the man!"* At that moment the cock crowed, and Peter remembered that Jesus had said, *"Before the cock crows, you will deny me three times."* (Matt. 26.75) Heartsick at what was happening to his beloved Teacher, and overcome by the guilt he felt at his repeated denial of Jesus, he fled, weeping bitterly.

THE FIRST TRIAL

This, the first of the trials, was a crucial step in the campaign to get rid of this troublesome rabbi who challenged the established authority at every step. The initial action, in the organized and well-orchestrated effort to eliminate the man, had been to question his authority when he taught in the temple. In this they had failed, while his popularity with the people had grown.

The objective here was to elicit testimony that would prove him to be a heretic, a blasphemer. It was a thinly veiled conspiracy that might also have failed had they not gotten from the mouth of Jesus himself statements that they chose to interpret as blasphemy. Under oath, he was asked, "*Are you the Messiah, the Son of God?*" Jesus knew that it did not matter what he said; their intent was to convict him. And when they asked him repeatedly if he was the Son of God, he replied, "*You say that I am.*" On this they convicted him, but it is important to note that he never said that he *was* the Son of God, and certainly not the *only* son. What he did say was of the utmost importance to every living soul. He said, "*But from now on the Son of Man will be seated at the right hand of the power of God.*" (Luke 22.69)

When Jesus used the term the *Son of Man*, he was *not* referring to himself alone, but to the essential nature of man *made in the image and likeness of God.* The *Son of Man* is anyone, man or woman, who has awakened to the nature of their personal relationship with God, that of a son or daughter to a wise and loving father. All who are fully aware of that relationship, as was the man Jesus, *know* that they are "*seated at the right hand of the power of God.*" It is this awak-

158

ening that the Master Teacher sought to bring about in his disciples, and in the whole of mankind.

For illustration of this power vested in the Son of Man, we need look no further than the reported episodes of healing that appear in the New Testament, for example the healing of the paralytic. (Matt. 9.2), "*And just then some people were carrying a paralyzed man lying on a bed. When Jesus saw their faith, he said to the paralytic, Take heart, son; your sins are forgiven.*" There were Scribes present who were heard to mutter, "*This man is blaspheming.*" Jesus, who was aware of their thoughts, said, "*Why do you think evil in your hearts? For which is easier, to say, 'Your sins are forgiven,' or to say, 'Stand up and walk'? But so that you may know that the Son of Man has authority on earth to forgive sins, he then said to the paralytic— 'Stand up, take your bed and go to your home.*" And the man stood up and went to his home. When the crowds saw it, they were filled with awe, and they glorified God, who had "*given such authority to men*" to mankind.

The truth is that we are not just human beings, we are spiritual beings, brothers and sisters with Christ, expressing and experiencing our humanity. Each of us is somewhere on that path from Adam to Christ, and the Bible provides us with a look at the terrain, while the story in which we are immersed suggests how we might successfully complete the journey.

That we, as the Son of Man, "*sit at the right hand of the power of God,*" is further illustrated in the lesson of the fig tree, and the words of the Teacher, "*Whatever you ask for in prayer with faith, you will receive,* for "*as you believe, so is it done unto you.*"

And when he healed the epileptic child who his disciples had failed to heal, Jesus said to the father of the child, "*All things are possible for the one who believes.*" (Mark 9.23) The child's father had cried out in frustration, "*I believe; Lord, help thou my unbelief!*" But there is no such thing as unbelief. What is present is a *belief* in failure. It is the same power misdirected. This is why on several occasions Jesus asked those who came to him for healing, "*Do you believe that I can do this thing?*"

And, of course, it was not unbelief that prompted Peter to deny Jesus three times on that fateful night; it was fear for his own safety. But no matter the reason, when *faith* (Peter) denies the Promise, whatever that may consist of, we are in that moment lost to the forces arrayed against us.

If the full import of what Jesus said had registered on the chief priest and elders, they would have realized that they faced a far greater threat than if he had just said that he was the Son of God. For with such an awakened mankind they, and their institutions, would become irrelevant. Jesus posed a threat to their very existence.

Jesus' Trial by Pilate

They were in agreement that the man must die but, being subject to the rule of Rome, they had no authority to carry out such a sentence. They had to devise a way to present a case to Pontius Pilate, the Roman governor that proved that Jesus was a threat to the rule of Rome, for only Pilate had the authority to issue a death warrant. So they bound Jesus and brought him before Pilate, where they accused him of *"perverting our nation, forbidding us to pay taxes to the emperor, and saying that he himself is the Messiah, a king."* (Luke 23.2)

The man who stood before him bound and bruised did not appear to Pilate to pose a threat to the might of Rome. With a barely perceptible grin tugging at the corners of his mouth he asked the man, *"Are you the king of the Jews?"* Jesus replied quietly, *"You say so."* (Luke 23.3)

It was obvious to Pilate that the crowd, led by their priests and elders, had their own problems with the accused that had nothing to do with Rome, and he had no intention of being drawn into their internal religious struggles. They were a stiff-necked, troublesome lot at

161

best. With a wave of dismissal he said, "*I find no crime in this man.*"

But the priests and elders were insistent in their complaint and said, "*He stirs up the people by teaching throughout all Judea, from Galilee where he began even to this place.*" When Pilate heard this, he asked whether the man was a Galilean. If so, then he was under Herod's jurisdiction, a man who Pilate considered to be a vicious pompous ass. With a look of satisfaction and relief, he said, "*Take him to Herod. He is in the city. Let him be the judge.*"

Herod was pleased when Jesus was brought Jesus before him, for he had long wanted to see him. He had heard reports of the man that spoke of miracles, and was hoping to see him perform some sign. He questioned Jesus at length concerning the accusations that the chief priests and scribes brought against him, and grew angry when Jesus stood silent.

Frustrated by Jesus' refusal to enter into the parody of justice that was taking place, Herod and his soldiers mocked him. "*A king of the Jews,*" they sneered, "*should be dressed in a manner to fit his lofty station,*" and placed a crimson robe on him, and sent him back to Pilate.

With the accused once more standing before him, Pilate summoned the chief priests, the leaders, and their followers, and questioned

Jesus yet again, saying, "*Are you the King of the Jews?*" Jesus replied with a question, "*Do you ask this on your own, or did others tell you about me?*" Surprised at the boldness of the response, and clearly annoyed, he barked, "*I am not a Jew, am I? Your own nation and the chief priests have handed you over to me. What have you done?*" (John 18.35)

Jesus replied, "*My kingdom is not of this world. If it were, my followers would be fighting to keep me from being handed over to the Jews.*" (John 18.36) Pilate asked him, "*So you are a king?*" Jesus answered, "*You say that I am a king. For this I was born, and for this I came into the world, to testify to the truth.*"

Pilate had heard enough. He looked quizzically into the eyes of the man before him, certain in his own mind that truth played no part in what had transpired here, and asked Jesus, "*What is truth?*" (John 18.38) Then he turned to the chief priests and elders, and the assembled crowd, and said to them, "*You brought this man before me charging that he was perverting the people. I have examined him in your presence and have not found this man guilty of any of your charges.*" He added, "*Neither has Herod, for he sent him back to us. This man has done nothing to deserve death. I will therefore have him flogged and release him.*" (Luke 23.15)

They took Jesus into the governor's headquarters, to an area set aside for flogging criminals. There they stripped Jesus of his robe, tied him to an upright pillar and administered the thirty-nine lashes that the sentence required. Each time the lash struck him his body convulsed against the bonds that held him, but not a sound issued from his lips. When the flogging ended blood poured from the wounds left by the lash, and his breath came is short rasping gasps as the entire company gathered around him.

Garrison duty could be a dull affair, and some of those who were off duty had already emptied several flasks of the sour wine that was a favorite among the troops. Always ready for a little fun, especially at the expense of one of these troublesome people, they replaced the scarlet robe that Herod had first put on him. Then they twisted some thorns into a crown which they jammed upon his head, and put a reed in his right hand as a scepter, and knelt before him laughing uproariously while they shouted, "*Hail, King of the Jews!*"

Through all this, Jesus stood impassive in their midst. Bloody trails from the crown of thorns embedded in his head, traced their way over his bruised face and into his beard. Dried spittle gathered in his beard and on the robe he wore like so many scabs from old wounds.

Throughout it all he remained silent, unmoved, and unresponsive, like the eye in the center of a storm. In the eyes of some of the hard-bitten legionnaires appeared a fleeting look of respect and, with even the most drunken of them the game had lost its edge. It was at that moment that Pilate summoned them to again bring Jesus before him.

Pilate was now well aware of the fact that the spurious charges brought by the Jews against Jesus were the product of fear and jealousy. And further, while he was conducting the trial he had received a request from his wife who asked that he have nothing to do with the man, Jesus, for she had the most troubling dream about him.

Jesus or Barabbas?

Now there was an established custom that during the festival the governor would release one prisoner, anyone that the crowd wanted. At that time they had a notorious rebel and murderer imprisoned, whose name was Jesus Barabbas. Pilate hoped that this would prove to be a way out of the troublesome situation he faced. He stepped out and stood quietly before the crowd until it became hushed, expectant. As ordered, his soldiers brought Jesus out to stand before the crowd. Pilate pointed to Jesus and said, "*Behold the man!*" (John 19.5)

Jesus robe that Herod's men had placed upon him lay like a hot blanket of pain upon his bruised and torn back. The thorns of the crown poked their hot, bony fingers into the flesh of his scalp. Utterly exhausted, he stood before them an object of ridicule, a living parody of royalty.

Pointing to Jesus, Pilate shouted, "*Whom do you want me to release for you, Jesus Barabbas, or Jesus who is called the Messiah?*" Surely, he thought, they would not choose Barabbas over an innocent man. But the chief priests and elders had done their work well. Their agitators, interspersed throughout the crowd, had skillfully played upon the emotions of the gathering, and had brought them to a fever pitch. Under their influence the crowd, now thoroughly conditioned, responded with shouts, "*Give us Barabbas.*"

In disbelief, Pilate asked them again, "*Which of the two do you want me to release for you?*" And they screamed, "*Barabbas!*" Pilate shouted, "*Then what should I do with Jesus who is called the Messiah?*" (Matt. 27.21) And they shouted as with one voice, "*Let him be crucified!*" Incredulous, he asked, "*Why? What evil has he done?*" But they shouted all the more, in a murderous chant, "*Crucify him! Crucify him! Crucify him!*"

During this exchange Pilate saw that as the crowd grew in size it grew more ugly, and he feared that he would soon have a riot on his hands. That would not play well with Rome. Why should he risk that? He had done what he could. But, so that all should know where he stood in the matter, he had a basin of water brought to him and, in full view of the angry mob, washed his hands before the crowd, and said, "*I am innocent of this man's blood; see to it yourselves.*" In response, an angry roar went up from those gathered, "*His blood be on us and on our children!*" (Matt. 27.24) Having washed his hands of the matter, Pilate released Barabbas to the crowd, and handed Jesus over to his soldiers to be crucified.

THE CHOICE

The trials lead inexorably to the condemnation of Jesus and ultimately to a choice between Jesus (the Christ), and Barabbas, (the rebel and murderer). When we consider how this choice is arrived at in the story, we may also catch a glimpse of how it plays out in the inner life of man.

Both Jesus and Barabbas were rebels, revolutionaries. As such, each posed a threat to the established way of things, but on different planes of living. Jesus' statement to Pilate, *"My kingdom is not of this world,"* gives us a clue. It was entirely predictable that the chief priests and elders, who represented the established religious structure, would choose Barabbas over Jesus. Barabbas' "kingdom" was very much of this world.

Barabbas was a revolutionary in the world. He posed a threat to the temporal rulers, in this instance Rome, but not to the religious or spiritual authorities. For their purposes he proved to be a useful tool. Barabbas had many followers, and his daring exploits against the rule of Rome had made him a hero to all who hated Rome but were afraid to raise their own voice, or hands, in acts of defiance. To Rome he was a mere gad-fly, but to the chief priests and elders he was the perfect foil for moving the crowd to call for his release instead of Jesus, when given the choice.

Barabbas was a hero to the common man, and was known to many more people than was the mysterious, wandering, rabbi from Galilee. It is likely that more than a few of his followers were numbered among the agitators within the crowd. Add to this, the strange attraction that the rebel has universally held for the common man in any society or time, and you see how useful Barabbas was to the chief priests and elders in this situation.

Jesus was also a revolutionary, but in the realm of spirit, of the mind and heart of the indi-vidual. He had brought his message to the very epicenter of the faith-based structure of Judaism — the temple. It was in that sacred space, which the chief priests and elders considered to be exclusively their very own, that he taught his revolutionary message of liberation. It was a message that pointed to a new relationship between man and God, a relationship like that of a son to a father. It was that the Son of Man (every living soul), is to sit at the right hand of the power of God. It was a threat of awesome proportions to the established religion, for it pointed to a complete replacement of the old by the new. Such a threat must not just be punished; it must be eliminated completely.

And we find the same dynamic at work in the inner life of man, each time a new vision, a new promise of liberation collides with the old, established way of being in the world. It is the clash that takes place in the mind of the alcoholic, or the drug addict, or anyone trapped in a downward spiral of life, when they awaken to the belief that a higher, more loving and joyous, way of being in the world is possible.

This will often occur when one has bottomed out, has no resources left and no place to hide. Someone once said that God puts one flat on his back in order to look into his face. It is at that moment that we turn to that sacred space within—the temple—and find the Teacher, with his message of liberation. But freedom is not to be had without a struggle.

For the moment the new and radical concept is born in the heart and mind, like the Christ-child in Bethlehem, it is locked in a struggle for its very life. It will be challenged, tried, and convicted by the established way of being in the world. And one or the other will be crucified; Jesus or Barabbas. It is our choice.

On reflection, how often do we call for Barabbas to be released and the Christ to be crucified? It is in the other choice that we are freed. It is the addiction, the bondage, whatever its nature that must be crossed out, crucified. We find in life that we often make the wrong choice, but do not despair. One thing is certain — you can always choose again.

It is by faith that we live, and move and have our being, and this is true even of the avowed atheist. We each live out our beliefs, *not* our opinions. If there is to be a change in our life, in our way of being in the world, it will *always* begin in the temple, the sanctuary of faith, repository of our beliefs. When the rebel appears in the temple, his very presence is a threat to the established belief structure. He will always be challenged as to his authority to be there, to teach there.

And the old established beliefs (the chief priests and elders) will use every device they can to discredit and condemn the new (the Christ, the Promise), for it must be killed in order for them to survive. They will first *arrest* the new, and their power will appear so overwhelming that faith in the new (Peter) will deny even knowing the Promise. They will gather witnesses to accuse the Promise of blasphemy, *heresy*, and will seek to condemn the Promise. But like the Jews under Roman rule, they are unable to impose a death sentence.

*Crucify him! Crucify him!
Crucify him!*

CHAPTER 14

Jesus Crucified

It was time to get on with the grisly business at hand. It was a duty that, with few exceptions, the soldiers universally detested. They were, after all, proud soldiers of Rome, not executioners. Most of them would rather face a brigade of the enemy than to take part in this duty, even when it was an enemy of Rome, like Barabbas, who was to be executed. Barabbas at least was a revolutionary, one who had led an insurrection against Roman rule, and in the process had killed Roman soldiers. But since it was only Rome that could condemn one to death, it was only the soldiers of Rome who could carry out the sentence.

The senior officer chose a young Centurion to be in charge of carrying out the sentence. He in turn picked twelve soldiers to form the execution squad. They stripped Jesus of all but a loincloth, and left the crown of thorns in place.

That done they formed up six on a side with Jesus in the center. With the young Centurion in the lead they left for Golgotha, the place of execution. In a storage area just outside the headquarters they selected a large timber for the crosspiece, and commanded Jesus to pick it up, and carry it. When the exhausted Jesus was unable to lift it to his shoulders, two soldiers picked it up and placed it on his back, and they marched him into the street.

They had not gone far, when Jesus staggered and fell to his knees. The soldiers helped him to his feet and continued on their way, but had gone only a short distance when once again Jesus fell prostrate upon the cobblestones. When it was clear that he would not be able to get up, or continue to carry the timber, they chose a burly bystander from Cyrene named Simon, who they compelled to carry the crosspiece.

The Passover crowd that filled streets quickly moved aside at the approach of the Centurion and his soldiers. As they made their way through the narrow, sun-drenched dusty streets, women cried and men cursed when they saw Jesus, and realized where they were taking him.

Even without the weight of the timber on his back Jesus staggered and fell several more times, on the way. His exhausted body moved, fell, got up again, and stumbled onward. It seemed somehow to be separate from him, a thing apart. Faces floated in and out of his vision, a woman's arm reached out, offering a piece of cloth for him to wipe the sweat and blood from his face. Gratefully he took it and wiped, and returned it to the extended hand. Taking it the woman gasped, for on it he had left an image, an unforgettable image.

They trudged onward and finally arrived at the place of execution, a hill called Golgotha, which means place of the skull. There were two felons already hanging upon crosses, and between them was a freshly dug hole in the earth. Lying upon the ground, with one end next to the hole, was a timber, longer than the one carried by Simon of Cyrene. With a great sigh of relief Simon dropped the crosspiece he had carried for the condemned Jesus, and was dismissed by the Centurion.

With a final glance at the still figure of Jesus, the man in whose footsteps he had walked through the streets of Jerusalem, Simon hastened to leave. He had no wish to witness anything more of this sad affair, nor any desire to remain one moment longer in this place of horror and death.

The soldiers secured the crosspiece to the upright, and then placed Jesus upon the cross, and spread his arms along the crosspiece and his body along the upright and nailed him to it by driving spikes through his hands and feet.

With each blow of the hammer a shudder of pain rippled through his body, each one building on the last, until he felt that he would surely drown in the agony. Finally the blows stopped, only to begin again when the soldiers nailed a plaque over his head that bore the legend, "This is Jesus, King of the Jews."

Then, sweating and grunting, the soldiers lifted the cross, with Jesus hanging upon it, and dropped the end of it into the hole with a sickening thud. A new wave of excruciating pain coursed through his body like liquid fire, he was barely able to catch his breath. The soldiers filled in the hole around the base of the cross. The weight of his body tore at the nails in his hands and feet; his arms were being torn from . their sockets.

THE CROSS

Although the cross is frequently associated with Christianity, and with this story, it pre-dates the suffering and death of Jesus by many hundreds of years. But it was during his time that its use as a method of execution became a common practice of Rome against its enemies, foreign and domestic, as both punishment and deterrent.

It was a most dreadful and torturous way to meet one's death, for it was not unusual for the condemned to take several days to succumb. In addition to the physical pain crucifixion was emotionally and mentally cruel for it stripped away every shred of dignity from the condemned, and left them exposed to the taunts and ridicule of the public.

The condemned was first flogged until the blood ran, or sometimes scourged, a more vicious and punishing use of the lash where pieces of metal or bone were attached to it. They were then required to carry the crossbeam to the site of execution, where their arms were tied to it, or in some instances nailed, with the spikes driven through the wrists. It was a slow and excruciating death, especially when they were tied instead of nailed, for the bonds cut off the circulation of blood, and the limbs became gangrenous. The practice was abandoned when the Roman Emperor Constantine converted and recognized Christianity as a state religion.

The cross as an instrument of execution appeared in several forms. The Roman version had the crossbeam about two-thirds up the perpendicular timber, while the Greek version has the two crossed at the center forming a plus sign, and St. Anthony's has the crossbeam placed on top of the upright like a T.

Whatever its form, it has for ages presented a mystical symbol of man and his existence upon the earth. When a person stands with arms outstretched we see the immediate resemblance; the image of a walking tree presents itself to our imagination. Symbolic of the human condition, the horizontal beam represents matter, the material world, while the upright symbolizes spirit, our divine nature. The point of intersection is in the area of the heart, where matter and spirit, the earth nature and the divine nature, join in the dance of life.

It is important to understand the symbolic nature of the cross in order to appreciate its relevance to the specific manner in which the man Jesus *must* die in the story. Had he met his death in any other fashion the story would lack this essential symbolic element, one that could not have been provided by any other means of execution.

There were other forms of execution used at the time of Jesus. The Greeks preferred poison, the Jews used stoning; it was only the Romans who crucified the offenders. It was necessary for Jesus to die in this manner, for only the cross could provide the necessary universal symbol of the death of man, and the release of the spirit. In a visual sense, spirit takes form by pouring itself into the upright of the cross, through the crown in man, and departs through the same point.

At birth every living soul is bound to the cross of physical existence, of life in this dimension, with its joy and its pain, its promise and its price. Each has his cross to bear. This presented a powerful metaphor that Jesus used in challenging those who would be his disciples, those who would enter upon his discipline. *"And he that taketh not his cross, and followeth after me, is not worthy of me."* (Matt. 10.38) *"If any man would come after me, let him deny himself and take up his cross daily and follow me."* (Luke 9.23) *"Whoever does not bear his own cross and come after me, cannot be my disciple."* (Luke 14.27)

Each of us must carry our *own* cross in life, for it is a symbol of life itself, the Word (Spirit) become flesh. And each life is unique in the cross it must bear, the challenges the soul has chosen for this life, and each is marked with a unique quality. One's particular challenge and the ability to meet that challenge combine to form the destiny of that soul's journey.

The burden may often seem to be unbearable, but if we look closely at any life to which we would attach the word greatness, it is abundantly clear that they have borne their own cross with dignity, and grace, and power. We will see that their cross, their unique burden, has

179

been a crucial element in the forging of that greatness.

Taking up one's cross and following the Christ is a choice made by a spiritual warrior; it is to enter upon the discipline of the enlightened one. Christ said, *"Take my yoke upon you, and learn from me."* He added, *"For I am gentle and humble in heart, and you will find rest for your souls."* (Matt. 11.29) We find rest for our souls when we meet the soul's demands, when we accept and respond to the challenge of our own cross.

The Two Thieves

Two thieves hung on crosses on either side of Jesus. One of them cried out in pain and anger, *"If you are who they say you are, why do you not save yourself? You're nothing. You're a fraud,"* The other pleaded, *"Remember me when you go to your Father."* Jesus told him *"Verily I say unto you today, you shall be with me in paradise."* (Luke 23.43)

THE THIEVES – A CLOSER LOOK

Two thieves were crucified with Jesus, one on the left and the other on the right. The one on the left "railed at him," screaming, "Are you not the Christ? Save yourself and us!" The other said to Jesus, "Jesus, remember me when you come into your kingdom." Jesus responded, "Truly, I say to you today, you will be with me in Paradise.

The two thieves are symbolic of the human condition in which the Christ is in the midst of them, in the present moment between the past and the future both of which are thieves. They always rob one of the full awareness of the present. The past often accuses and berates us for our perceived failures. It cries out to be saved from the consequences of its actions, while the future is quick to accept the promise of salvation.

They each rob one of the awareness of what is taking place in the moment, the only place where life is actually happening. The past often seems to die cursing, while the future seeks to extract a promise of salvation. Jesus' response, "I say to you today, you will be with me in Paradise," is one of several remarks spoken by Jesus from the cross.

*Forgive them Father they know not
what they do.*

CHAPTER 15

Words Jesus Spoke from the Cross

Through a red haze of pain he saw that the soldiers had moved away from the bottom of the cross, and were now drinking their sour wine and gambling over his robe. *"Forgive them Father,"* he gasped, *"they know not what they do."* (Luke 23.34)

His mother stood at the foot of the cross, her face twisted with horror and grief. Tears welled up in his eyes and mixed with the blood from the crown of thorns, as it traced its way down his face and into his beard. The love and sadness that gripped his heart was more painful than the spikes that impaled him on the cross. Standing next to her was John, the disciple he loved the most, and the only one present.

He looked into their uplifted faces, and in a loud whisper breathed, *"Mother, behold your son. Son, behold your mother."* (John 19.26)

He tried not to move, or even breathe, the pain was so intense. *"Eloi, Eloi, Lama Sabach-thani!"* He cried. *"My God, My God, why hast thou forsaken me?"* (Matt. 27.46)

The minutes seemed like hours, the hours like years. *"I thirst,"* he said. (John 19.28) A soldier placed a wine-soaked sponge on the tip of his spear and lifted it to his face. It was sour, bitter. He could not drink it.

He was vaguely aware of those who came to curse him; *"You who would destroy the temple and build it in three days, save yourself! If you are the Son of God, come down from the cross."* The priests, scribes, and the elders mocked him. *"He saved others; he cannot save himself. He is the King of Israel; let him come down from the cross now, and we will believe in him. He trusts in God; let God deliver him now, if he wants to; for he said, I am the Son of God."* (Matt. 27.42)

He let his mind go within, to drift down into the depths, away from the pain. But, no, in an ocean of pain, there was a sharp agony in his side. One of the soldiers had thrust a spear into his side to see if he is still alive, still conscious.

The hours passed, and finally he let go completely. *"Father, into thy hands I commit my spirit."* (Luke 23.46) And then, he drifted away from it all. *"It is finished!"* He whispered. (John 19.36) He saw his body still nailed in place on the cross, but he -- was free.

184

THE WORDS – A CLOSER LOOK

Nothing that appears in scripture is super-fluous. Everything included in the story is there for a purpose, and it is not just to move the narrative along, nor to fulfill prophecy, but to convey a larger meaning. The words that Jesus is said to have spoken from the cross, are no exception. (Note: There are seven statements in all, but they do not all appear in any one gospel.)

The first of these statements is made at the very beginning of the ordeal. Nailed to the cross, hanging on this tree of torture and pain, Jesus said, *"Forgive them Father, for they know not what they do."* Instead of cursing those who tormented him, he asked that they be forgiven, that they were acting out of ignorance. All such travesties grow out of Ignorance, the root of which is the mistaken belief in our separation from God, and from our fellow man. We have yet to learn that we are all expressions of the One, brothers and sisters, sons and daughters of the living God.

In Genesis 4.9, When Cain asked God *"Am I my brother's keeper?"* God might well have answered, "No! You *are* your brother."

Two thousand years ago this good, and in-nocent, man hung on a cross and asked God to forgive those who had nailed him there, and those who stood by to watch and mock him. Two millennia have passed, and one might well ask what we have learned? Little it seems, but do not despair, ignorance is not an incurable condition. The principle is, forgive and you will be forgiven; forgive not, and you will live in a poisonous atmosphere of your own creation.

To forgive others is a gift we make to ourselves, for it is we who experience the healing power of the act, and the release and freedom it brings. In the process we may learn to forgive ourselves of all the stupid, foolish, ignorant thoughts and actions of which we have ever been guilty, and there is nothing more vital to our mental, emotional, and spiritual health than that.

When we forgive ourselves we learn a significant piece of that truth that will make us free, and be assured that God, the Christ within, will not forever let any of us remain in darkness.

Among the faces that gathered around the foot of the cross, Jesus saw his Mother and his favorite disciple, John. To his mother he said, *"Woman, behold your son,"* and in the same breath, to John, *"Son, behold your Mother."* He knew that these two, whom he loved the most, would need the love and strength of such a relationship to face the days ahead. But his view of life and relationships was never this narrow.

On one occasion, when a group of followers was sitting around him, he was advised that his mother and brothers and sisters were outside, asking for him. He responded to this by asking,

"Who are my mother and my brothers?" Then looking at those seated around him, he said, *"Here are my mother and my brothers! Whoever does the will of God is my brother and sister and mother."* (Matt. 12.49) He taught that our essential relationship with each other is to be a nurturing, supportive one. It is well for us to remember that this includes our relationship with our internal mother, son, and daughter energy patterns, that they too be honored, nurtured, and supported as well.

Perhaps the most familiar words that he spoke were; *"Eloi, Eloi, Lama Sabachthani,"* commonly translated as, *"My God, My God, why hast thou forsaken me."* That which is a perfectly natural reaction for most, seems to have been a very strange and out-of-character statement for him to utter. From everything else he said, it was clear that he felt an intimacy with God, like that of a son to his father. Did he feel forsaken? (Note: this same cry is found in the opening sentence of Psalm 22.)

There are biblical scholars who, based on their study of the original Aramaic texts, suggest that this has been misinterpreted. For instance, the word sabachthani, at its root means *loosening, setting free, a cry of exaltation* (UMD p. 562). Was it a cry of frustration and despair, or exaltation? What are the implications of one or the other of these responses?

187

What is our response when we find our-selves in the midst of a painful experience that we did not consciously seek, or foresee—*nailed to the cross?* Do we cry out, "My God, my God, why hast thou forsaken me?" Or do we exclaim in exaltation, as perhaps Jesus did, "For this I came into the world. This is my chosen destiny?"

Who would choose the latter, it sounds masochistic? But in our life, as in the story, we always have a choice as to how we respond to what life presents to us. In the Christ story one translation is the cry of the victim, and the other is the shout of the victor. Since what is—is, and since what we name it we live with, the empow-ering response is to choose the role of victor.

It is not an easy choice, and many natu-rally choose the role of victim without realizing that in so doing they give away their power, the power of the *"Son of Man who sits at the right hand of the power of God."*

The opposite choice, the cry of an indomi-table spirit, is most clearly set forth in the following statement from *"A Course in Miracles."*

I am host to God, and hostage to no one, and to nothing. (5)

We often face this choice in life, and our response is a major factor in how we experience the event or circumstance. By our choice we name it, declare our perception of it, and then live with the nature of named—the context— rather than the content.

I thirst! Jesus cried. And a soldier used the tip of his spear to lift a sponge, dipped in sour wine and gall, to his lips. In his agony he might well have yearned for a sip of water or wine, but he could not drink that which they offered him. It is likely that the thirst he felt was for something more.

He might have thirsted for more people to understand and accept his message of forgiveness and love, or for Jerusalem, both the city and the state of man's mind, to be a place of peace instead of one of strife and weeping. He might have thirsted for people everywhere, people of every nation and every religion, to recognize their divine nature as sons and daughters of the One God. He might have thirsted for all people to remember that they are made in the image and likeness of God, by whatever name S/he is called. And thirsted for the day when the actions of all humankind would fulfill the two commandments he offered us to live by.

"Love God, with all your heart all your mind, and all your might; and love your neighbor as yourself." (Mark 12.30)

He might also have thirsted simply for an end to his agony in the flesh, and his return home to his Father. What is the nature of your thirst?

And finally, as the end approached, Jesus declared, *"Father, into thy hands I commit my spirit."* These words are also found in Psalm 31.5. Placed in that context they read.

Into thy hands I commit my spirit;
thou hast redeemed me, O Lord, faithful
God.

In truth our spirit is never out of God's hands, and yet in this act of surrender of the self we acknowledge and accept that Truth. More than that, in making this commitment we choose to consciously align our self, our purpose and actions, with the creative power and movement of that Truth. In making this commitment we become one with the Intelligence and Energy, the Power and Presence, that is the Source and Substance of all creation, that Power without which nothing exists, nothing happens—God, the Absolute.

When we fail to commit our spirit into the hands of the Father (God), we are become the Prodigal Son, he who decided that he could go it alone. His request was, *"Give to me mine inheritance,"* and it was given to him—as it is given to each of us. It was not very long before he found his resources depleted, his inheritance spent, and he was reduced to eating dry husks in the field. At which point he realized that even the servants in his Father's house were better cared for, and decided to return home.

Referring to God as Father, as was the practice of Jesus, is to point to a particular kind of relationship with God, one as intimate and nurturing as that of a loving father to a favorite son. It is to take that which is essentially inde-scribable, and absolute, and place it in a context around which the mind of man/woman can wrap itself.

Committing one's spirit into the hands of the Father in metaphysical terms is the placing of one's thoughts and actions, one's goals and objectives, into the crucible of God in action as Love and Law. All creation emerges from the interplay of these two forces, by whatever names you wish to call them—Energy and Intelligence, Feeling and Thinking, Yin and Yang.

Any action, any endeavor that we engage in without such a commitment of our Spirit, is doomed to failure. What we do in these in-stances may even appear to succeed in the eyes of the world, but in the absence of our commitment of spirit we will experience the result as empty husks.

When the spirit is not engaged the soul languishes and we, like the Prodigal Son, feed on the empty husks. An empty husk is that which is left over after the fruit or grain is gone, there is no nourishment left. The essence of life, the sweet joy of life has fled, like from the empty tomb, and to seek it there is to look for the living among the dead.

We would do well to begin each day, each action in pursuit of our soul's path, by declaring; Father, into thy hands I commit my spirit. By such a commitment we acknowledge the Source of all creation, and align our thoughts and actions with the Law—God in action. When we commit in this way, we follow the wise guidance found in Proverbs 16.2-3.

> "All the ways of a man are pure in his own eyes, but the Lord weighs the spirit. Commit your work to the Lord, and your plans will be established."

CHAPTER 16

Jesus Body is Laid in the Tomb

From the moment he was nailed to the cross, a darkness came over the land, and as he breathed those last words, *"It is finished!"* the earth shook beneath their feet. Rocks split and fissures appeared in the earth, and the *"veil of the temple was torn in two, from top to bottom."*

The Centurion and those with him, who stood at the foot of the cross, were utterly terrified. Ashen-faced, the young Centurion said, *"Truly, this was the Son of God!"* (Matt. 27.54) The women who had followed Jesus from Galilee, and provided for him, observed all this from a distance. Among them were Mary Magdalene, and Mary the mother of James and Joseph, and the mother of the sons of Zebedee.

Now there was a rich man named Joseph, from Arimathea, who was also a disciple of Jesus. He succeeded in getting an audience with Pilate, and asked that the body of Jesus be released to him for a proper burial, before the Sabbath commenced. Pilate was surprised, and wondered if Jesus was really dead in so short a time. It had only been three hours, while some felons had taken days to die on the cross.

He summoned the Centurion, who had overseen the execution, to see if he could confirm that Jesus was in fact dead. When the officer assured him that Jesus was dead, Pilate granted the request and ordered the release of the body to Joseph of Arimethea.

Joseph went at once to Golgotha, where he collected the body of Jesus, and removed the crown of thorns. He had the body taken to a tomb that had been prepared for his own burial, one hewn from solid rock. There he tenderly washed the blood from the body, and wrapped it in a clean linen cloth, and laid it in a prepared space. He had a huge stone rolled up against the entrance to the tomb and then left, for it was the day of preparation and the Sabbath was about to begin.

Mary Magdalene, and Mary the mother of Jesus, watched to see where Jesus was laid, and then they left to prepare the spices and perfumes to be used to properly prepare the body. The Sabbath began and they rested according to the commandment.

After the body of Jesus had been placed in the tomb, the chief priests and Pharisees sought an audience with Pilate to express their concern about the security of the tomb. They remembered that Jesus had said, *"Destroy this temple, and in three days I will raise it up again."* It was a statement that they took to mean that *"after three days I am to rise again."*

They asked Pilate to order that the grave to be made secure until the third day, for they feared that Jesus' disciples would come and steal the body away, and then declare that *"He has risen from the dead. This,"* they said, *"would make the last fraud worse than the first."* (Matt. 27.64)

But Pilate had endured enough of their whining fears, and their false charges, and dismissed them with, *"You have a guard; go, make it as secure as you know how."* They went and placed a guard over the tomb. They also *"set a seal on the stone."*

THE CRUCIFIXION PRINCIPLE

It is difficult to understand why an all-powerful, all-knowing, omnipresent God of love, would find it necessary to sacrifice a truly good and innocent man to atone for the sins of others. This question cries out for resolution, and it was the search for such, coupled with a growing love for the beauty, power, and wisdom found in the

Bible that prompted this current work. When one views the crucifixion through the lens of metaphor, it reveals a principle, a universal truth.

The Crucifixion, the crossing out, took place on Golgotha, which means *place of the skull*. It was here that Jesus met the final challenge that would fulfill the soul journey laid out for him at his birth. From his birth to his death, his life had followed a course that was seen as the fulfillment of the Messianic prophecy, a prophecy that could only be fulfilled by his death on the cross.

How much his personal choice played into these events, is a matter of conjecture. But it is clear that he could have avoided his trip to Golgotha had he chosen to do so. The choices that he did make could lead nowhere else.

Did he actually die on the cross, is a question that is bound to infuriate those faithful to the orthodox view. But the question is fueled by the scarcity of detail and other factors surrounding the execution and the handling of the body.

Pilate was suspicious enough to raise the question when approached by Joseph of Arimethea with a request for the body. He knew that Jesus had not been on the cross for more than about three hours, and that it was not unusual for the crucified to take days to die. He asked the Centurion, who had been in charge of the crucifixion, to confirm that Jesus was dead.

Something that perhaps he was not aware of was that the custom of breaking the felons legs to insure that they were dead, had not been carried out regarding Jesus.

The chief priests and elders were concerned enough to have placed a guard on the tomb. They knew that the disappearance of the body would lend credence to statements Jesus had made about "restoring the temple." To have this actually occur was their worst nightmare.

One might speculate that Jesus, in his travels during those *lost* years from age twelve to age thirty, had acquired a control of the physical body and its functions sufficient to feign death. But to believe that he would willingly submit to the agony of the cross in order to fulfill the Messianic prophecy requires a stretch of the imagination that is difficult to achieve. For those who love a conspiracy mystery, this one surpasses even the Kennedy assassination. But the scarcity of detail and, the unusual circumstances surrounding the death and disappearance of the body, were certain to raise the question.

Strangely enough, here we are not interested in facts, but in truth. If that sounds like a contradiction, it is not. When we view this 2000-year-old tale through the lens of metaphor, or myth, we see that it reveals a Principle, a universal truth, hidden within the fantastic narrative.

The principle revealed in the Crucifixion is one that is present in all of life, for all of mankind. It is reflected in the cycle of birth, death, and rebirth. There is always a dying of something for the new to be born. It is the upward spiral of life itself. It could be called the Resurrection Principle because, without the Crucifixion there can be no Resurrection.

When John the Baptist declared, *"I must decrease, and he (the Christ) must increase,"* it is the recognition of the awakening intellect, which resides in the skull (Golgotha), to the ascendance of spirit (the Christ) in the life. In the Crucifixion that ascendancy is carried to the ultimate, the personal will and ego are completely "crossed out" and replaced by Spirit, the Christ consciousness. It is a story of complete surrender to the reign of the Christ.

The Empty Tomb

As the first day of the week dawned, the women returned to the tomb bringing the spices and perfumes that they had prepared to anoint the body of Jesus. They found the stone rolled away from the tomb, but *"when they went in, they did not find the body."* (Luke 24.3)

They were astonished at the discovery, and knew not what to make of it. How could this be they wondered, when suddenly two figures in dazzling raiment stood beside them. The women were terrified and bowed their faces to the ground, but the men said to them, "*Why do you seek the living among the dead?*" (Luke 24.5)

They then reminded the women of what Jesus had predicted about his being delivered into the hands of those who would crucify him, but that on the third day he would rise again. The women remembered his words, and "*returning from the tomb, they told all this to the eleven and to others who were there.*" (Luke 24.9)

Their story was met with disbelief—an idle tale conjured up in the minds of grieving women. But Peter decided to check it out, and ran to the tomb. He stooped and looked in, and was amazed when he saw nothing but the linen cloths that had been used to wrap the body of Jesus, and nothing more.

You are witnesses of these things.

I send the promise of my Father upon you ... until you are clothed with power from on high.

CHAPTER 17

He Lives!

Now on that same day two men, among those who had followed Jesus, were going to a village called Emmaus, about seven miles from Jerusalem. As they walked along, talking about all the things that had happened, a man whom they did not recognize, joined them. When he asked them what they were discussing they asked him, "*Are you the only stranger in Jerusalem who does not know the things that have taken place there in these days?*" (Luke 24.18) When he asked them, *what things?* They replied, "*The things about Jesus of Nazareth, who was a prophet mighty in deed and word before God and all the people, and how our chief priests and leaders handed him over to be condemned to death. But we had hoped that he was the one to redeem Israel. Yes, and besides all this, it is now the third day since these things took place.*

Moreover, some women of our group astounded us. They were at the tomb early this morning, and when they did not find his body there, they came back and told us that they had seen a vision of angels who said that he was alive. Some of those who were with us went to the tomb and found it just as the women had said."

Then the stranger said to them, *"O fools, and slow of heart to believe all that the prophets have spoken! Was it not necessary that the Christ should suffer these things, and enter into his glory?"* (Luke 24.25) Then beginning with Moses and all the prophets, he spoke of all the scriptures concerning him, and they marveled at the depth and breadth of his understanding.

And when they drew near the village, which was their destination, it appeared that he intended to go on further. But they suggested that he stay with them, for the day was drawing to a close. He accepted their invitation and joined them at their evening meal. Here he took bread and blessed it, broke it and gave it to each of them; and their eyes were opened, and they knew him. With that he vanished from their sight. And they said to each other, *"Did not our heart burn within us, while he talked with us along the way, and opened to us the scriptures?"*

They could not wait, but returned at once to Jerusalem. There they found the eleven gathered together, and others who were present, and told them of meeting the stranger who was so well versed in the prophecies of the Messiah. They said that when he blessed and broke the bread, and gave it to them, they had finally recognized him as Jesus. They said, *"The Lord is risen indeed,"* and as they spoke, Jesus himself stood in the midst of them, and said to them, *"Peace be unto you."* Thinking that they had seen a ghost, they were terrified.

And he said to them, *"Why are you troubled? And why do these thoughts arise in your hearts? Look at my hands and my feet, and you will see that it is I myself. Touch me, and see for yourself; for a spirit does not have flesh and bones, as you see me have."* And he showed them his hands and his feet. Still they did not believe, and he said to them, *"Do you have any meat?"* And they gave him a piece of broiled fish, along with a piece of honeycomb. He took it and ate.

And he said to them, *"These are the words which I spoke to you, while I was yet with you, that all things must be fulfilled, which were written in the Law of Moses, and in the prophets, and in the Psalms, concerning me."* And with that he opened their understanding of the scriptures. He said, *"Thus it is written, and thus it was necessary for Christ to suffer, and to rise from the dead the third day, and that repentance and remission of sins should be preached in his name among all nations, beginning at Jerusalem."*

Then he added, *"And you are witnesses of these things and, behold, I send the promise of my Father upon you: but stay for a while in the city of Jerusalem, until you be endued with power from on high."* Then he led them out as far Bethany, where he lifted up his hands, and blessed them and parted from them, ascending up into heaven. (Luke 24.44)

While this was going on, the guards who had been assigned to watch over the tomb in which the body of Jesus had been laid went into the city and told the chief priests everything that had happened. The chief priests quickly assembled the elders, and devised a plan to pay the soldiers a large sum of money for their promise to say, *"His disciples came by night and stole him away while we were asleep."*

The guards agreed only after they were promised that should the matter reach the governor's ears, the chief priests would satisfy him and keep them out of trouble. Assured of this, they took the money and did as they were directed, and this version of story is still told among the Jews to this day.

THE RESURRECTION PRINCIPLE

Friday evening, before sunset, the body of Jesus was removed from the cross, wrapped in linen cloth and laid in a cave, a tomb hewn out of rock, and a huge boulder placed at the entrance. Early Sunday morning, some forty hours later, the women arrived at the tomb and found the stone rolled away, and the body gone. All that remained was the linen cloth in which the body had been wrapped.

This was the body of the man who thirty-three years earlier had been born in a stable, a place teeming with animal life force, where he was wrapped in swaddling cloths and laid in a manger. The Christ child was wrapped in swaddling cloths, symbolic of the confinement of spirit in flesh. The shroud, left neatly folded where the body of the crucified Jesus had been laid, is symbolic of a putting off of that confinement.

The tomb, a *cave*, with a huge boulder at the entrance, is a perfect symbol for the human heart when fear, doubt and ignorance (the huge stone) appears to confine the Christ within.

There is a popular painting that shows the figure of Christ standing outside the human heart and knocking at the door, seeking entrance, but it is the reverse that portrays the truth. Christ Universal, the Christ mind and Spirit, already dwells in every human heart. He stands inside the door knocking, seeking to lay aside the restraints, the wrappings, and emerge full-orbed into each life. When that stone is rolled away it is the answer to the Psalmist's prayer, *"Create in me a clean heart, O God, and put a new and right spirit within me."* (Ps. 51.10)

It is not by chance that it is the women who find the tomb empty. The woman, the carrier of life, would be the first to notice its absence. It is the feminine that cares for, and nourishes, the soul. It is an innocent, virginal, young woman who carries the seed of the Christ to its birth into the world, and it is the woman who seeks to attend the body when the Spirit has departed.

Neither the birth nor the Resurrection, each a transformation, can be brought about by the masculine energy. It requires the patient, passive, receptive soul-nature of the feminine to be the dominant energy. And with this in mind, we can see how both the cave and the manger are symbolic of the womb, each holding the seed of a new life.

WHY SEEK THE LIVING AMONG THE DEAD?

This is the question that the women are asked by a stranger in shining raiment, an angel, as they approached the tomb. The clear implication is that the man Jesus is not dead. We might pray that we be visited by an angel and asked the same question from time to time in life. If we are wise we will ask it of ourselves.

When a relationship has run its course and, like the empty tomb, there is no life or living left in it, and yet we attempt to resurrect it after the image of what might have been, we are engaged in seeking the living among the dead. In simple terms, when there is no spirit remaining in the situation, or the activity, and yet we persist in seeking what it once offered, or promised, we are seeking the living among the dead. The spirit has fled, and the *empty tomb* is a powerful symbol of the Resurrection principle. It is like the body after the spirit has fled, and like the empty chrysalis after the butterfly has flown.

"*He lives!*" The cry of wonder and astonishment reverberated around the known world. The man was dead, yet he lives. Huston Smith, in his popular volume, *World Religions*, asserts that it was this message more than anything else that gave impetus and growing acceptance to the new religion. The Resurrection! The promise of life after death, how mankind yearned for that message, and still seeks that assurance. To have *this* body rise from the grave, to resurrect it, like Lazarus, that was/is the hope.

We grow so attached to this body and its sensual experience, we are convinced that this must be the fulfillment of the promise of the Resurrection—of life ever-lasting. But the butterfly presents to the senses, to the rational mind, a clear and awesome example of the indescribable transforming power, and eternality, of Life Itself. But do we even begin to grasp the awesome truth of it?

How puny is our vision, how typically loaded with narrow limited expectations, when all we can conceive of is the resurrection of this particular body that we now inhabit. With the same rationale, if we were caterpillars our view of the Resurrection would be the vision of a more glorious worm. We seem to have no idea of the truly magnificent creation that Life has in store for us, a creation so free, so beautiful, that we would never have conceived of it in our wildest imaginings.

Is it not more likely, in view of what the caterpillar/butterfly transformation reveals that Life is an experience of ever-expanding glory, forever renewing itself? Is it not more likely that the Resurrection is not merely a rejuvenation of this body, but an entirely new creation? Spirit, God, is forever creating anew. There are no carbon copies, no retreads; every expression of life, every creation in all of eternity, is an original.

In truth, it is not a Resurrection. It is Spirit declaring with glorious imagination and enthusiasm, *"Behold! I make all things new."* The tree that brings forth leaves, blossoms and fruit this year, is not the same tree that brought forth leaves, blossoms and fruit last year, although it appears to be. That's why one can never step into the same river twice. Life is forever on the move. Creation, Genesis, is forever happening anew.

We see this renewal, this rebirth, most clearly every spring. All living things exhibit a new burst of Life. It is most graphic, most apparent, in those areas where trees and shrubs shed their leaves, and stand stark and naked under the onslaught of winter. They *appear* as though they are dead. One wonders whether they shall ever again be alive and vibrant in their coat of green, and one yearns for the return of spring, the renewal of Life.

However one views the Resurrection story, it is the eternal movement of Life, and it is *our* story. Do you yearn for the return of spring in your life? It has nothing to do with age you know. One can be in the midst of a cold, stark, barren winter experience at any age. It is at those times that we most need to remember the awesome transforming power of Life.

When we pass through the portal of death, Spirit departs the physical body only to take on the body of Light. Jesus, the Christ Universal, points the way but the upward spiral of life, the resurrection, is not the exclusive province of Christians, or of any particular religion or spiritual practice. It is the flowering of a seed of transformation imprinted in every human being, a spiritual DNA encoded in mankind at the moment of conception in the mind of God—it is inevitable. Sooner or later, we will each experience such a transformation.

THE STORY AND YOU

The story of the Christ points to a path, and to a goal, a prize. The path is the discipline that can move us to the discovery, and the nurturing, of that Christ seed within each of us. It is not an easy path, nor is any discipline that leads to a more abundant life here on earth, and to the Light beyond. But no soul is ever lost, no matter how afraid or sinful, or self-indulgent they might be.

They are like the song, "Looking for love in all the wrong places." But like the Prodigal Son, sooner or later they come to their senses, and turn homeward. And while they are yet a long way away, the Father sees them and delights in their return, and welcomes them with love.

The prize, the goal, is to *"have that mind in you"* that was in Christ, the Master Teacher. To which I would add, to also have that heart in you, for when the mind and the heart are joined in thought and act, wisdom is the result. And the premier quality of Jesus, the Christ, and of all the Master teachers who have trod the earth, is wisdom, that combination of heart and mind which is the highest expression of Love and Law.

And that wisdom is reflected in yet another quality present in each Master teacher, that of humility. Humility begins with the understanding that what we call *our* life is the One Life, God, expressing in, through, and as us. We did not create it. It is a gift, a precious gift, a goodly heritage. It is an inseparable piece of the movement of the great cosmic ocean of Life. And as awesome as that truth is, it lays upon each of us the task of picking up our own cross daily and carrying it with grace, and power, and dignity. Such is the path to the Universal Christ, and to the Resurrection.

Within this precious gift of life, hidden within the seed, is the creative power of Life Itself. We discover and acknowledge these gifts through the power of belief, and it is through our use of this power that we fashion our life experiences. *"As you believe, so is it done unto you."* All too often our belief is like that of the Prodigal Son, we are convinced that we are separate from the Source, separate from Life Itself.

This is like God playing a part in a theatrical production in which he is the Prodigal Son, and then forgetting that it is just a play. And in his forgetfulness, he experiences all the slings and arrows of that role. But God, as the audience, thoroughly enjoys the play in all its parts, for God is not just the Great Observer, but the Great

Experiencer, and you—are made in the image and likeness of That.

When we declare from our Christhood, *"The Father and I are one,"* and fully accept the truth of that relationship, we may come to realize that transformation is the very essence of the eternal creative play of spirit and matter in us, as us. This whirling dance is that of two halves of a Whole, opposite sides of the same coin, the eternal activity of the One—God. We are a process, a continual unfolding happening of Life itself, an integral part of an an upward spiral that is the evolutionary movement of consciousness in man. It is a movement of Life from darkness to Light, from ignorance to enlightenment, from Adam to Christ Universal.

The choice we face is whether to be an active or passive part of the movement. When we choose to pick up *our* cross and follow the Divine Example, we choose to be an active participant in the process. And when that is our choice it is as though all the forces in the universe move into alignment with it, and we find remarkable coincidences occurring in support of it. We meet kindred souls on the path who are actively engaged in the process, and we walk in each other's Light.

The story of the life of Jesus is the story of man evolving into the Christ. But revealing the Christ within requires more than lip service. The

Christ that awaits our recognition is not a cookie-cutter replica of Jesus, or a shifting of our sins to him for resolution and redemption. It is as the Buddha said to his followers; "With diligence work out your own salvation." Do the work. Accept the discipline. This is what the Master Teacher sought for all people. He did not set himself apart as the Great Exception, but lived—and still lives—as the Great Example.

He said, *"I am the light of the world."* (John 8.12) And without breaking stride said, *"You are the light of the world."* (Matt. 5.14) He declared, *"I am* (the Christ Universal) *the Life, the Truth, and the Way."* (John 14.6) When you and I can declare that truth as our own, and know it as the over-arching truth of this life that we live, we will have found the Christ within.

The great Persian poet Rumi, in *The Essential Rumi* (6), cautioned us not to be satisfied with just the name:

> *Don't be satisfied with the name of HU,*
> *with just words about it.*
> *Experience That breathing.* (p. 5)

> *Live in the one who created the prophets,*
> *else you'll be like a caravan fire left*
> *to flare itself out alone beside the*
> *road.* (p. 26)

The fateful journey did not begin with Jesus' triumphal entry into Jerusalem for the Passover; it began with his birth, as it does for each of us. He is one of a handful of souls whose lives have shed light on the journey that we each make. Each of us will take from the story such light as we are ready to receive. If we are truly wise we shall return to the story again and again for light upon our path. The open heart of a sincere aspirant will always find that particular ray of illumination that is needed, in the very moment that it is needed, until that day when the accumulated light will convince us of the truth of his statement. *I am the light of the world. You are the light of the world.* In that instant the anticipated Second Coming of the Christ will be realized.

God within me, God without,
How shall I ever be in doubt?
There is no place where I may go
And not there see God's face, not know
I am God's vision, and God's ears.
So through the harvest of my years
I am the Sower and the Sown,
God's Self unfolding and God's own.
Author Unknown

REFERENCES

1.   Lindsell, H. (1983) *The Holy Bible – New and Old Testaments – Revised Standard Version.* Grand Rapids; Zondervan Corporation.

2.   Thompson, F. *The Hound of Heaven.* Mt. Vernon; Peter Pauper Press.

3.   Franck, F. (1976) *The Book of Angelus Selesius.* New York; Random House.

4.   Wing, R. L. (1986) *The Tao of Power.* New York; Dolphin Book Doubleday.

5.   *A Course in Miracles.* (1980) Foundation for Inner Peace. Famingdale, N. Y.; Coleman Graphics.

5.   Barks, C. (1997) *The Essential Rumi.* Edison, N.J.; Castle Books.

6.   Johnson, R. A. (1989) *He: Understanding Masculine Psychology.* New York; Harper & Rowe.

7.   Johnson, R. A. (1989) *She: Understanding Feminine Psychology.* New York; Harper & Rowe.

8.   *Metaphysical Bible Dictionary.* (1966) Unity School of Christianity.   Lee's Summit, Missouri.

ABOUT THE AUTHOR

Edward V. Tuttle has been a minister for nearly thirty years. What began as an avocation in 1973 became a full time occupation in 1983. His ministry falls within that uniquely American religious movement known as New Thought, sometimes referred to as practical Christianity, which first appeared at the beginning of the twentieth century. *Sacred Stories, Sacred Dreams: Bible Myth and Metaphor* was born out of years of study and contemplation from that perspective, together with the principles of dream interpretation. He now devotes himself full-time to writing and counseling, and lives in Santa Maria, California, with his wife Linda, a mental health professional.

Printed in the United States
706400002B